PLAN FOR
NEW HAVEN

FREDERICK LAW OLMSTED JR.

AND CASS GILBERT

PLAN FOR
NEW HAVEN

Preface by Vincent J. Scully
Introduction by Alan J. Plattus
Afterword by Douglas W. Rae

TRINITY UNIVERSITY PRESS
San Antonio, Texas

Published by Trinity University Press
San Antonio, Texas

New cover design and book composition by
Barbara Aronica-Buck and David Wilk for Booktrix (www.booktrix.com)

The original interior of this book was produced in 1910. It is reproduced here as a
facsimile edition lacking only the original map that was tipped into the book in its original edition.

Trinity University Press strives to produce its books using methods and materials
in an environmentally sensitive manner. We favor working with manufacturers that
practice sustainable management of all natural resources, produce paper using recycled stock,
and manage forests with the best possible practices for people, biodiversity, and sustainability.
The press is a member of the Green Press Initiative, a nonprofit program dedicated to
supporting publishers in their efforts to reduce their impacts on endangered forests,
climate change, and forest-dependent communities.

The paper used in this publication meets the minimum requirements of the
American National Standard for Information Sciences—Permanence of Paper for
Printed Library Materials, ANSI 39.48-1992.

Library of Congress Cataloging-in-Publication Data

Olmsted, Frederick Law, 1870–1957.
[Report of the New Haven Civic Improvement Commission]
The plan for New Haven / Frederick Law Olmsted Jr. and Cass Gilbert ; Preface by Vincent J.
Scully ; Introduction by Alan J. Plattus ; Afterword by Douglas W. Rae.
p. cm.
ISBN 978-1-59534-129-7 (pbk.)
1. City planning—Connecticut—New Haven. I. Gilbert, Cass, 1859–1934. II. Scully, Vincent,
1920– writer of added commentary. III. Plattus, Alan J., writer of added commentary. IV.
Rae, Douglas W., writer of added commentary. V. Title.
NA9127.N4A3 1910a
711'.4097468—dc23
2012002216

16   15   14   13   12   5   4   3   2   1

CONTENTS

PREFACE

PLANS OF NEW HAVEN

by Vincent J. Scully

New Haven's first plan was a sacred one. It began with Ezekiel[1] when, Jerusalem destroyed and lost, God brought the prophet to a high place: "In the visions of God he brought me into the land of Israel, and set me upon a very high mountain, by which was as the frame of a city on the south."

For John Davenport that mountain was East Rock. Down below it was the harbor, the haven, indeed the New Haven for fugitives from the old world. The city Davenport laid out between the mountain and the harbor was exactly as described by Ezekiel and drawn up from that description several times during the Middle Ages (upon which all the plans of the great Spanish cities of the New World were based), but most recently by the Spanish monk Juan Bautista Villalpando in 1604. It was published in Rome with many illustrations and would have been, of all the plans, the one best known to Davenport. It was a perfect square divided into nine smaller squares and with twelve gates, each held by one of the tribes of Israel, with the Levites divided into four to guard the tabernacle in the central square. This became Davenport's Green, with the meetinghouse in the center, facing east because, as Ezekiel says, "The glory of the God of Israel came from the way of the east."

Villalpando's plan shows all of this, as does Davenport's, its streets generated by Villalpando's gates. It is oriented with east below, west above, as was Villalpando's. And all of the major plans of New Haven over succeeding centuries were oriented this way, as if obeying God's injunction to Ezekiel to see to it that the new inhabitants held in every way to these sacred forms: "And write it in their sight, that they may keep the whole form thereof, and all the ordinances thereof, and do them."

Davenport's plan, so derived, was unique in the English colonies, while ubiquitous, at least as a square grid, in the Spanish. But the grid plan as such, also found in Philadelphia and Savannah, became the basic plan of America's expansion across the continent, though with the great green normally squeezed out of it by the demands of commercial real estate. But the size of New Haven's square plan seems of special significance. It is about a five-minute walk from the periphery to the green, and for the Garden City and City Beautiful planners of the period around 1900 this came to be regarded as the ideal size for a neighborhood. Moreover, the New Urbanists of the present day, who are in many ways reviving Garden City and City Beautiful traditions, believe the same, so that Davenport's plan takes on another significance as a kind of perfect model of pedestrian scale.

As such a model, the nine squares, though having been subdivided around 1800, were probably at their most perfect around 1910. By this time the meetinghouse had long been succeeded by three churches facing east, while the green was defined by the high escarpment of Yale along its western edge and embellished as well by the classical buildings of the City Beautiful movement: the free public library, the county courthouse, and the post office. Most of all, the rest of the nine squares had been solidly built up so that the green became a majestic void, an expansive open space in the center.

But the architects of the City Beautiful movement also had something else in mind: the extension of the pedestrian city by dynamic movement through and beyond it, a vehicular concept soon seized upon but not wholly dominated by the automobile. Hence the grand boulevard of George Dudley Seymour's proposal, a lively diagonal linking the new railroad station with the old nine squares. But it was a park as well as a roadway, for pedestrians as well as for cars, and derived from the great avenues of L'Enfant's Washington and the City Beautiful plans that emulated it, most spectacularly Burnham's proposals for San Francisco and Chicago.

Behind them all was the royal tradition of the French classic garden, especially that of Versailles, with its leafy allées leaping beyond the horizon to carom off other étoiles, so shaping the image of the new France as a nation at continental scale and in truth with a cosmic order. So the boulevards assert the human control of a world meant to be traversed, one that was eventually to be torn apart by the automobile. But in Seymour's proposal the boulevard still perfectly complemented the green and connected its pedestrian scale with the transcontinental scale of the railroad. Its objective was the glorification of mass transportation, not of the automobile. The redevelopment of the 1960s literally destroyed all that. Appropriately enough, its Oak Street connector, embodying the triumph of the automobile over pedestrian and railroad alike, brutally severed the connection between the green and the station, cutting right through the proposed area of Seymour's boulevard. It is equally appropriate that the connector is now scheduled for destruction, but it is surely sad that the boulevard was never built at all. Its presence during the critical decade of the sixties might well have made its significance manifest even to the planners of redevelopment, so that the connector might never have been built as it was.

Now, in the beautiful plan drawn by Erik Vogt,[2] we can see how decisively well the boulevard would have worked for the city as a whole, and how spectacular it would have been if Bertrand Goodhue's City Beautiful plan for Yale of 1919 had been accepted by the university. In that case, connected through the green by Temple Street, the new diagonals of town and gown would have transformed the center of New Haven into a great park expanding out from the center toward the railroad on one side and, on the other, Science Hill. Again, it was an unfulfilled dream of urban grandeur, a lost vision of what city and university together might have been.

But such splendid visions never really die, and the very first plan produced by the New Urbanism, that for Seaside, Florida, of 1980—designed by Andres Duany and Elizabeth Plater-Zyberk, graduates of Yale's architecture school and students of New Haven—was like a hymn of gratitude to this city. The grid is there, and the diagonal avenues, all in a compact little town. They are perhaps more than the plan requires, but they are a statement of vitality and of future achievement and, most of all, a celebration of their parentage.

---

1 The relation to Ezekiel was first noted by John Archer in "Puritan Town Planning in New Haven," *Journal of the Society of Architectural Historians* 34, May 1945, 140–49. The relation of the plan to the landscape was soon realized, and the whole story has been most richly explored by Erik Vogt in "A New Heaven and a New Earth: The Origin and Meaning of the 'Nine Square Plan,'" in Vincent Scully, Catherine Lynn, Erik Vogt, Paul Goldberger, *Yale in New Haven: Architecture and Urbanism* (New Haven, 2004), 37–51.

2 Scully et al., *Yale in New Haven*, 225.

INTRODUCTION

THE 1910 NEW HAVEN CIVIC IMPROVEMENT COMMISSION REPORT AND THE AMERICAN CITY PLANNING TRADITION

by Alan J. Plattus

The report prepared by Cass Gilbert and Frederick Law Olmsted Jr. for the New Haven Civic Improvement Commission, submitted to the secretary of the commission, George Dudley Seymour, on February 21, 1919, and then presented by Seymour to New Haven mayor Frank J. Rice on September 26, 1920, is a crucial document in the history of American cities and city planning. Just a year before, the Plan of Chicago, prepared by Daniel Burnham and Edward H. Bennett, had appeared, establishing the high-water mark of the City Beautiful movement, which could be said to have begun in Chicago sixteen years before with the World's Columbian Exposition, the so-called White City, also organized by Burnham. And in the same year, the first national conference on city planning had been held in Washington, D.C., at which many of the themes and concerns that motivated professional planners then, as the field was taking shape, and still do today were articulated. None other than Frederick Law Olmsted Jr. delivered the keynote address in which he situates the need for planning in the context of the social and environmental degradation of the rapidly growing industrial cities of American free market capitalism.[1]

The 1910 Plan, as it is usually called, straddles the somewhat overstated divide between the first era of modern American urban planning in the years after the Civil War, beginning with the Parks movement led by Frederick Law Olmsted Sr. and most often identified with the City Beautiful movement led by Burnham, Bennett, Charles Follen McKim, and others, and the succeeding era of progressivism, professionalization, and the so-called City Practical.[2] The first era was very much part of an intellectual and practical sea change that was transforming the way in which western cities were understood and designed, beginning with the mounting critique of the industrial city in the first half of the nineteenth century, with Carlyle, Pugin, Ruskin, Engels, Marx, and many others, and culminating with the replanning of Paris, Vienna, and Barcelona from the 1850s on. The United States was not far behind, with Olmsted and Vaux winning the competition for the design of Central Park in 1859 that launched their practice. Of course, European cities, and Paris in particular, would be the gold standard for modern urbanism in the United States all through the second half of the nineteenth century, a reference point somewhat obliquely reflected in the illustration of Budapest as an example by the authors of the 1910 Plan.

With the transition to the City Practical, or "City Functional and Scientific," and professionalized planning in the first decades of the twentieth century, German and English practice gradually replaced Paris and Rome as touchstones—at least, for the new field of city planning. Many of the key figures in the latter development turn out to have been landscape architects by training, like John Nolen and Frederick Law Olmsted Jr., who founded the first professional planning practices, as distinct from planning, urban design, and "civic art" projects undertaken within architectural practices. Not surprisingly, those practices can be more easily, if not entirely accurately, seen to grow out of the Parks movement, and, indeed, a large part of those practices, and a powerful paradigm for American planning as a discipline, involves parks and park systems, including parkways, with campus planning and garden suburbs as a growing component, already staked out as specialty by the original Olmsted firm. Almost equally influential, however, are the social reformers, like Jane Addams of Hull House and the settlement house movement in general, who, like the Olmsteds senior and junior, saw open space not simply as an aesthetic embellishment of a well-planned city but as necessary to the health and social development of city dwellers, particularly new immigrants and the urban working class.[3] Thus the dominance, after traffic and circulation, of parks and open space as an issue for the 1910 Plan.

The fact that traditional architects like Cass Gilbert are still seen as integral to the team for a project such as the 1910 Plan points to the artificiality of the notion of a real epistemic or institutional break at this point and to the modernization of architectural practice, to include not only the houses and commercial establishments of the civic and corporate elite but also an already growing component of city and campus planning, and eventually housing as well. Cass Gilbert probably remains best known for his pioneering Manhattan skyscraper for Frank Woolworth of 1910–13 (right after the New Haven Report was submitted), or for monumental Beaux-Arts public buildings like the earlier Minnesota State Capitol (1895–1905) or the U.S. Supreme Court Building completed in 1935, after Gilbert's death. And yet both of those public buildings were, in principle, parts of ambitious planning schemes that demonstrate the extent to which Gilbert saw individual buildings as integral to larger ensembles, if not entire cities, and also as opportunities, both conceptual and professional, to stake out and articulate those larger fields. This aspect of Gilbert's practice has received more attention recently, and there is no better illustration of the relationships in question and how they usually played out in practice than his work in New Haven.[4]

The built legacy of Cass Gilbert in New Haven, and the principal artifacts of the 1910 Plan other than the report itself, are two public buildings: the New Haven Public Library facing the green at the intersection of Temple and Elm Streets, and Union Station about a mile away, still in use and beautifully restored as the Amtrak and Metro North station. Gilbert had probably begun both before, and certainly very early in, the process of work on the 1910 Plan. He was to meet and work with the principal instigator and organizer of the whole civic improvement movement in New Haven, George Dudley Seymour, through these two projects.[5] Indeed these buildings, which seem so distant and disconnected today, were to be the effective anchors of the most monumental and characteristically City Beautiful features of the 1910 Plan: a grand avenue leading from a polygonal plaza in front of the new station, connecting to a new public square at the southern edge of the original nine squares of New Haven and ingeniously resolving the complex intersection of the station avenue, Congress Avenue, and Temple Street; the latter would be widened as a new central axis crossing the green, where it would meet the new library on the green's northern edge.

The architecture of these two buildings was to have signified their respective roles in the plan and their relationship to the city and its history. The public library was designed as a highly original reinterpretation of conventional Beaux-Arts classicism to reflect the colonial, really Federal, architecture of the green, in particular David Hoadley's United Church on the Green just across from the library. Seymour and Gilbert had ambitions that the library would be an integral part of a larger scheme of monumental public buildings around the green's northeast corner. The report also illustrates a train station with an enormously monumental rusticated Roman triumphal arch frontispiece, although Gilbert tried other styles, including Georgian, before building the elegantly spare neo-Renaissance prism that still stands in search of its unrequited plaza and avenue.

Like so much of City Beautiful movement monumental planning—the Cleveland Group Plan by Burnham, John M. Carrere, and Arnold W. Brunner (1904); Burnham and Bennett's San Francisco Plan (1905); Gilbert's own plan for the area around the state capitol in St. Paul (1906); or for that matter Burnham and Bennett's 1909 Chicago Plan—the 1910 New Haven Plan was realized only in fragments, and it was more fragmentary than most. The exception that proves the rule may be the ongoing influence of the 1901 McMillan Commission Plan for Washington, D.C., an effort led by Burnham and McKim, which of course built upon the already grand framework established by Pierre-Charles L'Enfant in 1792. There one can see in Burnham's Union Station and its role in the plan the sort of thing Gilbert had in mind for New Haven. Even in the monumental heart of Washington, D.C., however, one can observe over time the characteristically American tension between the design of individual buildings and previous planning ideas that each of those buildings inevitably reinterpret and even challenge, as Gilbert himself did in his (unsuccessful) struggle to revise what he considered the inauspicious siting of his building for the Supreme Court, inherited from the 1901 Plan. That tension, which has provided one of the central themes in the history of American architecture and urbanism, and which was particularly crucial to the debates around the time of the 1910 Plan as planning attempted to liberate itself from, and then to assert control over, the traditional role of architecture, is certainly lurking behind one of the main premises of the 1910 Plan: the need for collective responsibility and action to temper the worst effects of individualism.[6]

Both the underlying need for the report and its ultimate recommendations are predicated on two related premises, one empirical and the other ideological. The ideological premise, with its strong sense of urban order (and, of course, disorder) as a manifestation of the fundamental moral order of the body politic, ties the 1910 Plan not only to the moralizing aesthetics of the City Beautiful movement but also to much older strains of thought in the history of architecture and urbanism. These connect the apparently superficial boosterism of the City Beautiful, and the bosses and businessmen who sponsored it, to the classical tradition as filtered through Renaissance and Enlightenment theory and practice, the latter having provided the staples of the precedent-based education of Beaux-Arts–trained architects like Charles McKim. On the other hand, the empirical premise, which logically sets the stage for the ideological position of this and other contemporary plans, has at least one foot planted firmly in the world of the emergent fields of urban sociology and statistically based social science, even if that foot turned out to have been set down in quicksand rather than scientific bedrock. Indeed, Gilbert and Olmsted, most likely the latter (no doubt with the encouragement and assistance of Seymour), made a point of their engagement of a Yale College senior "specializing in social and statistical science," one Roland M. Byrnes, to provide a detailed sociological analysis, a "statistical picture," of New Haven in 1908. While most of that work was relegated to an appendix with little direct relation to the main body of the report, the main demographic analysis produced by Byrnes, of population growth and diversification, was central to the argument.

Many of the plans put forward in this era were predicated upon bold forecasts of continuing dramatic population growth and diversification. The 1909 Plan of Chicago, for example, cited the forecasts of the engineer and planning consultant Bion J. Arnold, who projected Chicago's population in the year 1952 at 13.25 million, when in fact it peaked at around a quarter of the predicted number.[7] The peculiar method employed by Byrnes to project New Haven's population growth, using the actual growth curves of other American cities, produced strikingly similar results: a population predicted to triple and reach 400,000 by 1950; in fact, the population peaked around that time at about 165,000. These understandably exaggerated projections, which were produced well before the automobile and other factors changed the geography of American population distribution in ways that could not have been easily imagined at the height of the streetcar era in 1910, by no means invalidated the plans' recommendations, which were, in any case, largely aimed at addressing existing conditions even as they warned of the need to plan for more dramatic future growth. More importantly, they set the stage for a further escalation of the verbal and spatial rhetoric of an approach to planning predicated on continued explosive urban growth, which, by the postwar years, fueled by polemics and proposals developed in the white heat of prewar European avant-garde urbanism, saw the earlier plans of Burnham, Bennett, Gilbert, and others as not nearly bold enough, just as many older urban centers like New Haven were beginning to hemorrhage population and jobs.

Be that as it may, it is the undeniable documentation of a growing and, perhaps more importantly and provocatively, rapidly diversifying urban population that leads directly to the report's second, ideological, premise. This premise is not only a fundamental principle for the emergent discipline and profession of city planning, as it sought to define itself in relation to the hitherto laissez-faire growth of modern American cities; it is also profoundly, even radically, political, as the authors clearly realized. It is articulated in the report's first paragraph:

New Haven has not only been growing at a steadily increasing rate, but . . . many of those now living will see the completion of the process by which it is being transformed from the pleasant little New England college town of the middle nineteenth century, with a population of relatively independent, individualistic and self-sufficing householders, into the widespread urban metropolis of the twentieth century, the citizens of which *will be wholly dependent upon joint action for a very large proportion of the good things of civic life.* [my emphasis]

Having taken this stand, the authors are immediately defensive, as so many planners and progressives still seem to be, about the possible specter of "socialism" but then just as quickly and unapologetically reassert the inevitability of "increasing mutual dependence" in the tasks of civic improvement. Convincing civic and business leaders, not to mention politicians and ordinary citizens, of this new agenda and its urgency in the context of the early years of the Progressive Era was in many ways as challenging a task for the authors and sponsors of the 1910 Plan as the technical issues addressed by the plan. The introductory letter by the committee secretary, George Dudley Seymour, notes that, leading up to the submission of the report, the Yale School of Fine Arts had sponsored a lecture series on the need for civic improvement, including talks by Cass Gilbert on grouping public buildings, Olmsted Jr. on parks, and other notable architects.

In the end, all the things that the early planners attempted to counteract—individualism, laissez-faire development, and good old practical politics and patronage—got the better of the 1910 Plan and its promoters, in the short run, at least.[8] Charles Seymour, who would campaign indefatigably for the plan and its principles for the rest of his life, was in the end bitterly disappointed, and although New Haven, still very much in the vanguard of American cities, got both a City Plan Commission in 1913, with Seymour as secretary once again until he finally quit in disgust in 1924, and a zoning ordinance (only three years after New York's pioneering ordinance of 1916), real comprehensive city planning as it was conceived by Olmsted Jr., Seymour, and all the other pioneers of that generation would only truly arrive, and then like a massive hurricane, with the election of Richard C. Lee as mayor of New Haven in 1953, and the advent of urban redevelopment. By then much had changed, including planning models, architectural typologies and style, the incipient loss of industry, and the impact of the automobile and suburbanization, not to mention political rhetoric and the growing influence (eventually) of community organizing and resistance. In retrospect, the bustling industrial city of 1910 must have seemed almost genteel, with its slow-moving mix of early automobiles, streetcars, horse-drawn carts, and pedestrians, and with its Civic Improvement Committees, "manned" mostly by the prosperous, white-male descendents of the old New England civic elite, with factory owner Max Adler and theater mogul Sylvester Z. Poli thrown in as, it turns out, an anticipation of the radical changes the plan was seeking to encompass and direct. And yet the story of citizen-led planning and the vision of a connected city of parks, parkways, and boulevards articulated by grand civic buildings perhaps no longer looks as quaint as it may have at the time of the plan's fiftieth anniversary.

NOTES

1 See Richard E. Foglesong, *Planning the Capitalist City: The Colonial Era to the 1920s* (Princeton, 1986), 3–4.

2 This distinction is already part of the rhetoric of the times. Indeed, the term "City Practical," as an alternative and challenge to "City Beautiful," may well have originated with Cass Gilbert. In the historiography of American planning, the distinction is made structural by Mel Scott's influential anniversary history of planning, *American City Planning since 1890: A History Commemorating the Fiftieth Anniversary of the American Institute of Planners* (Berkeley, 1969), and it remains a central feature of most historical treatments, cf. e.g., Jon A. Peterson, *The Birth of City Planning in the United States, 1840–1917* (Baltimore, 2003), usually with the more or less explicit message that the City Beautiful was an aesthetically based movement led by architects, while the modern profession of city planning is a scientifically based and socially and politically responsive field led by "planners."

3 See Galen Cranz, *The Politics of Park Design: A History of Urban Parks in America* (Cambridge, MA, 1982).

4 See especially the work of Barbara S. Christen, "The Architect as Planner: Cass Gilbert's Responses to Historic Open Space," in Margaret Heilbrun, ed., *Inventing the Skyline: The Architecture of Cass Gilbert* (New York, 2000), 177–228; and "A 'New' New England: Proposals for New Haven and Waterbury, Connecticut," in Barbara S. Christen and Steven Flanders, eds., *Cass Gilbert, Life and Work: Architect of the Public Domain* (New York, 2001), 177–91.

5 For the details of these commissions and the relationship between Gilbert and Seymour, see Christen, "A 'New' New England," op. cit. 179–84.

6 On this dialectic and its role in the formative period of American planning and architecture, see Mario Manieri-Elia, "Toward an 'Imperial City': Daniel H. Burnham and the City Beautiful Movement," in Giorgio Ciucci, Francesco dal Co, Mario Manieri-Elia, and Manfredo Tafuri, *The American City: From the Civil War to the New Deal* (Cambridge, MA, 1979). It makes the interesting argument that the American tradition of romantic individualism shapes the relatively autonomous buildings of Sullivan (and later Wright) and is challenged by Burnham, whose later buildings are always implicitly part of a larger urban idea. One might add, following Christen's analysis of Gilbert's work in New Haven and Waterbury, Connecticut, that he would fall squarely into the Burnham camp.

7 Carl Smith, *The Plan of Chicago: Daniel Burnham and the Remaking of the American City* (Chicago, 2006), 35.

8 For this part of the story, see the afterword by Douglas Rae.

SELECTED BIBLIOGRAPHY

Original Sources

Burnham, Daniel H., and Edward H. Bennett, *Plan of Chicago* (Chicago, 1909).

———, *Report on a Plan for San Francisco* (San Francisco, 1905).

Burnham, Daniel H., John M. Carrere, and Arnold W. Brunner, *The Group Plan of the Public Buildings of the City of Cleveland* (Cleveland, 1903).

Ford, George B., "Recent City-Planning Reports," *National Municipal Review* 1 (April 1912), 262.

Gilbert, Cass, and Frederick Law Olmsted Jr., *Report of the New Haven Civic Improvement Commission* (New Haven, 1910).

Hegemann, Werner, and Elbert Peets, *The American Vitruvius: An Architect's Handbook of Civic Art* (New York, 1922).

Robinson, Charles Mulford, *The Improvement of Cities and Towns* (New York, 1901).

Seymour, George Dudley, *New Haven* (New Haven, 1942).

Secondary Sources

Boyer, Christine, *Dreaming the Rational City: The Myth of American City Planning* (Cambridge, MA, 1983).

Cedro, Rico, *Modern Visions: Twentieth-Century Urban Design in New Haven* (New Haven, 1988).

Christen, Barbara S., "The Architect as Planner: Cass Gilbert's Responses to Historic Open Space," in Margaret Heilbrun, ed., *Inventing the Skyline: The Architecture of Cass Gilbert* (New York, 2000), 177–228.

———, "A 'New' New England: Proposals for New Haven and Waterbury, Connecticut," in Barbara S. Christen and Steven Flanders, eds., *Cass Gilbert, Life and Work: Architect of the Public Domain* (New York, 2001), 177–91.

dal Co, Francesco, "From Parks to the Region: Progressive Ideology and the Reform of the American City," in Giorgio Ciucci, Francesco dal Co, Mario Manieri-Elia, and Manfredo Tafuri, *The American City: From the Civil War to the New Deal* (Cambridge, MA, 1979), 143–291.

Draper, Joan E., *Edward H. Bennett: Architect and City Planner, 1874–1954* (Chicago, 1982).

Fishman, Robert, ed., *The American Planning Tradition: Culture and Policy* (Washington, D.C., 2000).

Foglesong, Richard E., *Planning the Capitalist City: The Colonial Era to the 1920s* (Princeton, 1986).

Kohler, Sue, and Pamela Scott, eds., *Designing the Nation's Capital: The 1901 Plan for Washington, D.C.* (Washington, D.C., 2006).

Krueckeberg, Donald A., ed., *Introduction to Planning History in the United States* (New Brunswick, 1983).

Manieri-Elia, Mario, "Toward an 'Imperial City': Daniel H. Burnham and the City Beautiful Movement," in Giorgio Ciucci, Francesco dal Co, Mario Manieri-Elia, and Manfredo Tafuri, *The American City: From the Civil War to the New Deal* (Cambridge, MA, 1979), 1–142.

Osterweis, Rollin G., *Three Centuries of New Haven, 1638–1938* (New Haven, 1953).

Peterson, Jon A., *The Birth of City Planning in the United States, 1840–1917* (Baltimore, 2003).

Rae, Douglas W., *City: Urbanism and Its End* (New Haven, 2003).

Reps, John H., *Monumental Washington: The Planning and Development of the Capital Center* (Princeton, 1901).

Schaffer, Daniel, ed., *Two Centuries of American Planning* (Baltimore, 1988).

Scott, Mel, *American City Planning Since 1890: A History Commemorating the Fiftieth Anniversary of the American Institute of Planners* (Berkeley, 1969).

Smith, Carl, *The Plan of Chicago: Daniel Burnham and the Remaking of the American City* (Chicago, 2006).

Wilson, William H., *The City Beautiful Movement* (Baltimore, 1989).

REPORT OF THE

NEW HAVEN CIVIC IMPROVEMENT COMMISSION

CASS GILBERT, Architect

FREDERICK LAW OLMSTED, Landscape Architect

TO THE

NEW HAVEN CIVIC IMPROVEMENT COMMITTEE

NEW HAVEN

DECEMBER, 1910

THE NEW HAVEN CIVIC IMPROVEMENT COMMITTEE

OFFICERS.

To His Honor Frank J. Rice, Mayor of New Haven:

Dear Sir:—I have the honor to present herewith the report of Mr. Cass Gilbert and Mr. Frederick Law Olmsted of a plan for the development of New Haven.

This report is the result of a movement started by an "Open Letter" published by the subscriber in the issues of the New Haven "Register," "Union," and "Leader" for June 5th, 1907. Following the publication of the "Open Letter," the Hon. John P. Studley, then Mayor of New Haven, called a mass meeting of citizens to be held in Colonial Hall on the evening of June 19th, 1907. This meeting was largely attended and great interest in the project discussed by the letter was shown. The following resolution, offered by Henry C. White, Esq., seconded by Burton Mansfield, Esq., and endorsed by several of our most prominent citizens, was unanimously passed:

"*Voted:*—That a committee be appointed by the Mayor, of which he shall be a member *ex officio*, to include one member of the Board of Aldermen, one member of the Board of Park Commissioners, and nine other citizens, to employ experts to prepare a plan for the improvement of the city of New Haven, if after consideration they deem this course advisable; to procure, by appropriation or otherwise, the money necessary to pay the charges and expenses of such experts, if employed; and to bring any plan which may be made to the attention of the government and people of the city, with the committee's recommendations in regard to such plan; said committee to have power to add to and fill vacancies in its membership."

In pursuance of the above resolution, Mayor Studley within a few days appointed the above New Haven Civic Improvement Committee, barring Mr. Poli, whose name was added by the Committee at a meeting held October 7, 1907, in order that our Italo-American citizens might be represented. The Committee met for the first time in the Mayor's room on July 1st, 1907, and at that time decided to invite Mr. Cass Gilbert and Mr. Frederick Law Olmsted to prepare a report upon the improvement of the city, and to ask citizens of known public spirit to subscribe the sum of ten thousand dollars ($10,000) to defray the expenses of securing and publishing the report of the experts. This appeal was made through circulars and the press, and about eight thousand dollars ($8,000) was within a few weeks subscribed without resort to personal solicitation, by the persons and firms whose names appear in the appended list. The subscriptions were nearly all in the amount of one hundred dollars each.

Mr. Gilbert and Mr. Olmsted began without delay to collect the material for the report, and in this they were cordially assisted by city officials and public spirited citizens. To rehearse the details of the preparations required and to describe the data collected would require a book in itself. Mr. Gilbert and Mr. Olmsted repeatedly visited the city to collect material and familiarize themselves with its particular requirements, for cities are as individual as men. Mr. Olmsted kept one of his trained assistants here for several weeks examining the topography of the environs of the city and making sketches for maps. To assist Mr. Olmsted on the sociological side of the work the Committee employed Mr. Roland M. Byrnes, who was then a member of the senior class of Yale University, specializing in social and statistical science. From official and other sources Mr. Byrnes gathered together a vast amount of material, which he embodied in a report submitted in February, 1908. So valuable is this "statistical picture" of New Haven as it was in 1908 that it has been condensed and printed as an appendix to the report.

The material having been collected, it yet remained to study it—to consider what recommendations should be made and at length to prepare plans and maps, and to write the text of the report itself. The report now is presented to the public for discussion, and for adoption. It is hoped that its recommendations will be seen to be well considered, to conform to the best modern practice in this country and in Europe, and calculated to develop and extend in the most rational way, and for the good of the largest number of people, the plan of the city which had for its basis the historic "nine square" plan as adopted by the founders of New Haven in 1638.

Respectfully submitted,

GEORGE DUDLEY SEYMOUR, <i>Secretary,</i>

New Haven Civic Improvement Committee.

New Haven, Connecticut,
    Sept. 26, 1910.

Note: It should be stated that on the initiative of Professor John F. Weir, director of the Yale School of the Fine Arts, the Trowbridge Lecture Course, the season of 1907–8, was given in connection with the movement for civic improvement. These lectures, open to the public, were given in the Trumbull Gallery of the Art School building. The following is a list of the speakers, their subjects, and the dates on which the lectures were given:

December 3, 1908, Mr. Frank Miles Day, president of the American Institute of Architects, "Civic Improvement in the United States"; December 10, 1908, Mr. Cass Gilbert, A.I.A., S.A.R., "Grouping of Public Buildings"; December 17, 1908, Mr. John M. Carrère, A.I.A. (of Carrère & Hastings), "Civic Improvement as to Parks, Streets and Buildings"; January 21, 1909, Mr. Walter Cook, trustee of the American Institute of Architects, "Some Considerations in Civic Improvement"; January 28, 1909, Mr. Frederick Law Olmsted, Jr., A.S.L.A., "Parks and Civic Improvements"; February 4, 1909, Mr. Charles Howard Walker, A.I.A., "Embellishment of Cities."

LIST OF SUBSCRIBERS TO THE FUND FOR SECURING THIS REPORT.

Max Adler
Harry W. Asher
Samuel R. Avis
Judge Simeon E. Baldwin
S. H. Barnum
John K. Beach
Thomas G. Bennett
Hon. Frederick A. Betts
Edward F. and Frederick C. Bishop
Hon. Edward A. Bowers
Hon. Dennis A. Blakeslee
Henry Brewer
Frederick F. Brewster
Prof. George J. Brush
Dr. William H. Carmalt
D. G. Carmichael
Hon. Minotte E. Chatfield
George W. Curtis
Leonard M. Daggett
Harry G. Day
Charles S. DeForest
John I. H. Downes
Rev. Dr. Timothy Dwight
Rev. Robert J. Early
Henry F. English
Lewis H. English
Henry W. Farnam
Thomas W. Farnam
William W. Farnam
Hon. Frederick B. Farnsworth
   (Mayor of New Haven, 1897-1899)
Prof. Irving Fisher
John B. Fitch
Gamble-Desmond Co.
Frederick D. Grave
George E. Hall
James Hillhouse
Prof. Yandell Henderson
George E. Hodson
Thomas Hooker

Hon. George F. Holcomb
   (Mayor of New Haven, 1885-1887)
Henry L. Hotchkiss
Frederick J. Kingsbury, Jr.
Walter E. Malley
Hon. Burton Mansfield
John T. Manson
Judge A. McClellan Mathewson
Rev. M. McKeon
Ralph Miner
Gen. Phelps Montgomery
James T. Moran
Charles H. Nettleton
Hon. Henry G. Newton
Henry F. Parmelee
Frank W. Pardee
William S. Pardee
Sylvester Z. Poli
Prof. Edward V. Raynolds
   (Died January 26, 1910)
Edwin P. Root
Henriette F. B. Root
Prof. Edward B. Reed
Leoni W. Robinson
Amory E. Rowland
Lucien Sanderson
Prof. John C. Schwab
George Dudley Seymour
Henry M. Shartenberg
Judge Earnest C. Simpson
Prof. E. Hershey Sneath
Levi T. Snow
Rev. Anson Phelps Stokes, Jr.
Hon. Nehemiah D. Sperry
Edward S. Swift
Sherwood S. Thompson
   (Died August 7, 1907)
Frank W. Tiernan
Henry H. Townshend
Winston J. Trowbridge

FRANK D. TROWBRIDGE
ARTHUR B. TREAT
THE TUTTLE, MOREHOUSE & TAYLOR CO.
WILLIAM R. TYLER
  (Died September 25, 1907)
VICTOR MORRIS TYLER
JULIUS TWISS
COL. ISAAC M. ULLMAN
CHARLES M. WALKER
CURTIS HOWARD WALKER
PROF. GEORGE D. WATROUS

PIERCE N. WELCH
  (Died October 26, 1909)
HENRY C. WHITE
HON. ELI WHITNEY
WEIBEL BREWING CO.
DR. F. H. WHITTEMORE
HON. ROLLIN S. WOODRUFF
  (Governor of Connecticut, 1907-1909)
ARTHUR B. WOODFORD
MARGARET C. WOODFORD
YALE BREWING CO., INC.

THE REPORT OF THE
NEW HAVEN CIVIC IMPROVEMENT COMMISSION.

BROOKLINE, MASSACHUSETTS, February 21, 1910.

MR. GEORGE DUDLEY SEYMOUR, *Secretary*,

    NEW HAVEN CIVIC IMPROVEMENT COMMITTEE,

        NEW HAVEN, CONNECTICUT

Dear Sir:

In accordance with your request we have prepared a preliminary report upon the improvements of the City of New Haven as outlined in our letter dated August 2, 1907, in which we wrote in part:

"In a project of this importance it is desirable to proceed in a tentative and conservative way, especially at the outset. It would seem best therefore that a preliminary study should be made which would show only the general conditions that may be found to exist, without carrying the matter into any extended detail.

"We must prepare ourselves to meet the questions and the criticism that will inevitably arise, and it may be necessary to go into these and other like matters perhaps farther than either the Committee or ourselves can now foresee. While the purpose of the project is the preparation of a plan that will preserve and perpetuate the beauty of the city and suggest lines of further development for its future growth, we all realize that such a plan must be *practicable* as well as *beautiful*, or it will fail to commend itself to the community. The preliminary work then is of great importance and will take time and labor proportionately.

"We would visit New Haven as necessary to get the facts, going over the ground personally, aided by such maps as we presume to be now in existence, which would show the streets and parkways, location of principal buildings, public and private, and other data needed. We would then prepare a preliminary report which would express in general terms the recommendations which might appear to us proper and accompany this with illustrations or suggestions in sketches and photographs. . . . This would give an opportunity for a discussion of the preliminary report, which would undoubtedly bring out valuable suggestions, and after conference with your Committee and with the Municipal authorities we could agree as to what part, if any, of the project could be reasonably undertaken, and if so determined we could then proceed to develop the design and submit it with a full report containing a final recommendation."

We have spent much time studying the problems of New Haven and have gone far in the actual preparation of the full report proposed, in order that we might make our preliminary report with more confidence and more accuracy.

The accompanying report we beg to submit for discussion and approval.

Very truly yours,

Cass Gilbert

Frederick Law Olmsted

CONTENTS.

CONTENTS.

PRESENT CONDITIONS AND TENDENCIES.

The citizens of New Haven are familiar with the fact that the city is growing rather rapidly and that it is changing character as it grows; but many of them fail to realize how rapid and how profound these changes are likely to be in the near future. A consideration of the accompanying diagram, No. 1, will convince anyone that New Haven has not only been growing at a steadily increasing rate, but that many of those now living will see the completion of the process by which it is being transformed from the pleasant little New England college town of the middle nineteenth century, with a population of relatively independent, individualistic and self-sufficing householders, into the widespread urban metropolis of the twentieth century, the citizens of which will be wholly dependent upon joint action for a very large proportion of the good things of civic life.

Whatever views may be held by anyone upon the subject of socialism in its controversial aspects, there is no escaping the fact that the normal course of urban development through which New Haven is passing leads inevitably to an increasing mutual dependence, and that just as surely as the earlier stages of this development force the installation of a joint water supply, a joint sewer system and a constantly increasing outlay for improving the streets upon which the urban travel is concentrated, so surely also will the conditions of a dense and widespread population force the joint provision of other facilities which the experience of large cities has proven to be necessary for the well-being of their people.

For these reasons it is important not only to consider what is needed for the proper performance of the functions now imposed upon streets and parks and the whole physical equipment of the municipality, but also in a great measure to forecast the inevitable demands of the future greater city.

In order to estimate what the future character and extent of the city will probably be, it is needful to consider its past and to compare it with cities that have gone through a similar history and already reached greater development.

At our suggestion Mr. Ronald M. Byrnes has made a careful compilation of statistical information concerning New Haven and each of its several wards. The full text of his interesting and valuable report, forming a statistical picture of New Haven, is appended hereto; and only the broadest of the conclusions to be derived from it will be now considered.

Growth of Population.

The matter of first importance is the population. The accompanying diagram shows the five-fold growth of New Haven since 1850. It also shows for comparison the growth curves of certain larger cities so placed upon the diagram that the point in each curve representing a population of 108,000 is made to coincide with the point in the New Haven curve representing the census of 1900, when its population was 108,027, and plotted at such a scale that the curves will fall practically parallel to that of New Haven. A comparison of these curves before and after passing the 108,000 mark suggests the probable doubling of the present population of New Haven in about the next twenty-five years, and a population of some 400,000 by the year 1950. In the absence of radical and unexpected changes in economic and social conditions, such as to interrupt the world-wide phenomenon of steady urban development, it is more likely than not that the end of the twentieth century will find New Haven Green the center of a metropolitan population of about a million and a half, substantially the situation of Boston Common to-day. This is a

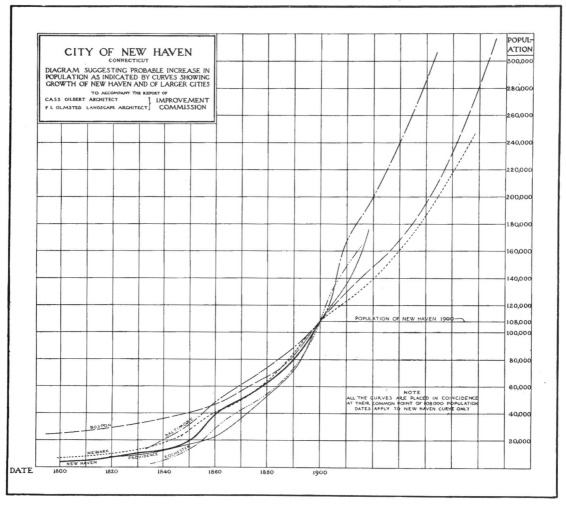

No. 1. Growth in Population.*

fairly long look ahead, but it is to be considered that a large proportion of the most important existing thoroughfares of New Haven were laid out more than a hundred years ago; that the great majority of streets and parks, once laid out and surrounded by buildings, will have to be made to serve their functions without substantial change of location or size not merely for a hundred years but for centuries unnumbered, and that worthy and beautiful buildings, from every period when such buildings were erected, have outlasted many centuries, and after many adaptations to new uses still contribute to the dignity and beauty of the noblest cities of to-day. In those improvements which are of permanent effect it would be folly for the city to ignore the requirements of this great future population.

* According to the Federal Census of 1910 the population of the City of New Haven was 133,605.

Composition of Population.

The composition of New Haven's population as to nativity is graphically shown in the accompanying diagram, No. 2. The city has obtained about one-third of its increase in population through immigration. The Irish, although still predominating among the foreign born in 1900, were actually decreasing in numbers, while the more recent immigrants from southern and eastern

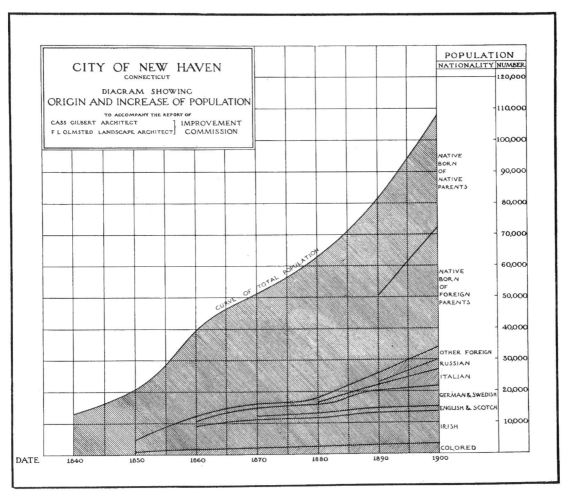

No. 2. Composition of Population.

Europe bid fair soon to overtake the older sources of foreign population and probably to increase materially the total percentage of foreign born in the city. Moreover, the birth rate of the Italians and Russians is strikingly higher than that of the earlier immigrants, that of all the immigrants is higher than that of the native born, and that of the native born of foreign parents is greater than the rate of births among native parents. Therefore it is clearly evident that the percentage of old New England stock in the population is progressively diminishing. People of the old New England stock still to a large extent control the city, and if they want New Haven to be a fit and worthy place for their descendants it behooves them to establish conditions about the lives of *all* the people that will make the best fellow-citizens of them and of their children. The racial habits and traditions, the personal experience and family training, the economic conditions and outlook, of the newer elements of the population, are such that a *laissez faire* policy applicable to New England Yankees is not going to suffice for them.

Economic Basis of Growth.

The basis of New Haven's growth and its economic support is fortunately varied;—it is not a one-industry town; it is a local distributing center, a local coastwise shipping port, an educational center of national importance; but its chief economic resource appears likely to remain light manufacturing of various sorts. The climate, the situation, the natural surroundings of the city, are such that people here can work hard and enjoy life.

It is the duty of the city to conserve these natural advantages and so to control its development that the man-made conditions of living and working—the housing, the transportation, the sanitation, and all the rest of it—shall make possible the greatest productive power along with the greatest satisfaction in the work and life.

Physical Conditions.

Physically the city has changed within the lifetime of the present generation from a New England country town, where one could readily walk from the small business nucleus near the Green, under arching elm trees and between detached houses set in gardens, to the surrounding open country. By carefully picking the route, by shutting one's eyes occasionally to the surroundings and by walking a sufficient distance, it would be not impossible to do the same to-day in certain directions; but the chances are few and are destined to disappear altogether. The elm trees have practically disappeared from the downtown streets and are rapidly being killed off elsewhere, while little serious effort is made to maintain them; two-family and three-family houses and tenement blocks are already numerous and are increasing; the open country is being driven beyond ordinary walking distance for the average man,—to say nothing of women or children; and the average distance traveled by each citizen going to and from his work and his recreation is becoming so great that street travel is increasing much faster than the population, and the dependence of the people upon street railway facilities has already become almost as complete as in the greatest centers of population; as shown by the fact that, in the year 1907, the number of street railway passengers in New Haven reached a total of 31,599,453—about 243 rides per capita.

Dwellings are spreading in almost every direction where the topography and transportation facilities permit, and within more restricted limits industrial establishments are similarly spreading.

The most important transportation route of all, the main line of the New York, New Haven & Hartford Railroad, has recently been improved at great expense, to increase its capacity for the rapid and efficient dispatch of traffic, and plans have been thought out for other enlargements of railroad facilities in and near New Haven; but the streets over which must pass practically all the local traffic by street cars and otherwise are no wider than was thought desirable and proper for the little New England town. Not only have the old town streets remained unwidened, as was natural, but also the same old standards have been thoughtlessly applied to the thoroughfares along which the new city is pushing itself out into the open farm land.

In the matter of recreation facilities the city has acquired for permanent preservation some notable vantage points, and has begun to provide local parks and playgrounds; but acquirements have been made only in an unsystematic way and New Haven has not fairly faced the problem of the modern democratic city, which is to provide means for healthful recreation within the reach of *all* its people now and for all time. The natural opportunities for outdoor recreation afforded by the varied topography of the region around New Haven are admirable and can be kept so, if brought under proper public control, as is possible under a well-directed policy of conservation.

No. 3.   Heart of the City as it was in 1824, when the main streets were still ample in width, and the countryside was within easy walking distance.

Financial Conditions.

We are not in a position to discuss the financial condition of the city, but the facts for a series of years, in regard to assessed valuations, indebtedness and tax rates, are given in Mr. Byrnes's report. In comparing these figures with those of other cities, or in drawing deductions from them, it is necessary to take account of the varying ratios between assessed and actual values of real estate (personal property assessments, of course, are so incomplete as to be meaningless) and to take account of the value of the lands and public service equipments owned by the city. For example, the whole waterworks system, including large reservations of land on the watersheds, is owned, not by the public, as in the case of Hartford, Boston, Providence, and New York, but by a private company whose capitalization is naturally not represented in the city debt.

So far as appears on the face of the figures, there seems to be no reason why New Haven should hesitate, on the score of financial difficulties, to undertake a bold and farsighted policy in needful public improvements, provided the work is done without extravagance, waste or corruption.

KINDS OF IMPROVEMENT MOST NEEDED.

The modern city is the product of improved transportation and one of its most vital concerns is its transportation system; for long-distance traffic the railroad and the harbor serve, but for local traffic the network of streets and street railways is almost the sole reliance.

While the problems of harbor and railroad development are of the utmost fundamental importance, so far as concerns any practical steps that the city needs to take they are so little pressing that we shall touch on them very briefly before taking up the main thoroughfares and street railway lines. We shall then touch in order upon: street trees, poles and wires, advertising signs, local streets, the sewerage problem, local parks and playgrounds, rural parks and reservations, and parkways. Still other improvements might be mentioned, but this list includes those for which prompt and comprehensive action seems most needed.

The Railroad.

The chief factor in the transportation system is of course the main line of the New York, New Haven & Hartford Railroad. With the recent improvements this may fairly be assumed to be a permanent fixture. A new and adequate station is already planned, and its location, determined by operating requirements, has also been definitely fixed. The local freight service of the railroad is carried on at the central yard, near the station, and at sidings along the main line and its branches, especially the short branch with many sidings that supplies the factory district of Mill River. The central yard with its connecting piers covers a large area and can be still further enlarged by filling out into the harbor. The freight yard of the Berkshire Division seems relatively unimportant, so near the main yard, and will probably be diverted to other uses. A small yard may be needed in the westerly part of the city, and if so, will probably be located in that part of the West River valley where the connection between the Berkshire Division and the main line now occurs. One feature of the railroad system not sufficiently provided for, that will need development, is increased yard space and sidings for factories. From every point of view the best locality for the chief development of that sort is in the valley of the Quinnipiac River. To the northeast or leeward side of the city, on the marshes of the Quinnipiac east of the Hartford Division, is a great extent of flat land, cheap, well adapted for freight yards and factory sites, and paralleled by a ridge of high land on the west where operatives' houses can spread to advantage. Houses so placed would be within comfortable walking distance, not only of the main line of the railroad and the factories that may be erected along it here, but of the State Street car line, which is probably the most important line of local transportation of the industrial district.

The Harbor.

In earlier days the prosperity of New Haven grew largely out of its shipping trade, and, while the importance of water transportation, as compared with rail transportation, has declined under the action of a complex set of causes to a very minor position in New Haven to-day, the example of Europe and the basic economy of water shipments seem to indicate that its importance is likely to increase again in the future. The United States Government may be relied upon to deal with the maintenance and probably with the improvement of the harbor channel, but it is more than questionable whether the development of wharfage will take place in such a way as to encourage greatly the growth and improvement of general facilities for water shipment, if the harbor frontage is occupied and developed mainly by the railroad and by individual manufacturing concerns and dealers; so that, without some form of public control, the great value of the water front in city development as well as for purposes of recreation is likely to be wasted or lost.

Many of the foreign cities control their shore properties. New York has gained possession of, rebuilt and leased most of her docks and is increasing her holding of undeveloped shore front. Chicago has started upon a tremendous enterprise in shore improvements in adopting and working upon a plan to build a chain of islands, piers and bridges along the whole lake shore. New Orleans has remarkably successful municipal wharves. Under conservative management New Haven could well afford to gain possession of the greater part of her entire water front, and, after reserving a few points for pleasure resorts, gradually develop or lease for development under proper supervision the pier and dock facilities along the harbor front within the limits marked by Sandy Point and Fort Hale Park. On the shores of the outer basin beyond these points, where commerce will probably never be able to use any considerable areas, many charming tracts should be preserved forever as public resorts.

Main Thoroughfares and Car Lines.

It is hardly necessary to discuss the vital importance of adequate thoroughfares for local transportation. The economy and convenience with which people may carry on all their activities in a city are perhaps more dependent upon the efficiency of the street system than upon any other part of the municipal plant, and it is certain that no other part of that plant is as difficult to enlarge or radically to alter when it becomes inadequate for growing needs. When in addition it is considered that the street system involves by far the largest financial investment under city control, equivalent to the ownership of a fifth to a third of the land area in fully developed sections, and that the cost for street improvement and maintenance is one of the largest items in the city budget, and that the cost is largely determined by the plan of the streets, it is surprising that the street layout should be left so largely to chance and to the initiative of individual landowners as it has been in the past. Probably the greatest defect in the New Haven street plan, as in that of most American cities, arises from the failure to recognize that a relatively small number of streets, on account of their locations, grades and other considerations, are bound to carry the major part of the traffic; that these main thoroughfares need to be very much more capacious than the average street and that local streets which are likely to carry but little traffic other than arises from the property abutting upon them may profitably be made a good deal narrower than the average street.

Practically every main thoroughfare will have a car line in it, and practically every street of considerable length having car tracks in it is thereby made a thoroughfare of importance. Main thoroughfares may vary in type from the ordinary city street of respectable width to the broadest layout having separate roads for heavy teaming and for pleasure travel, or for slow vehicles and for fast ones, and having a separate right of way for electric cars, shaded promenades for people on foot and other special features, with perhaps a more or less parklike character for the sake of incidental recreation.

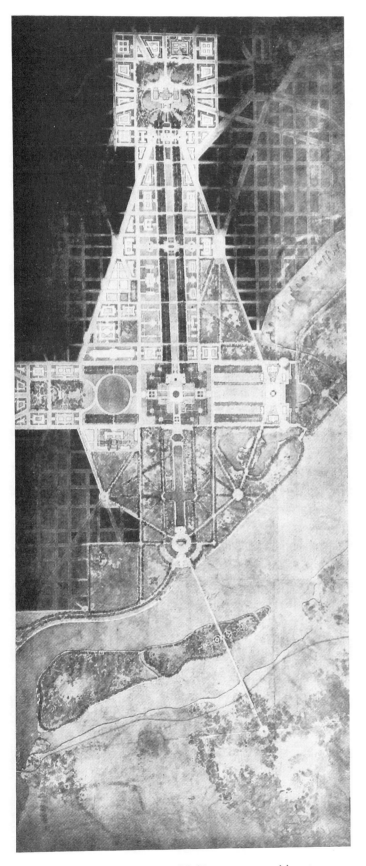

No. 4. Plan for the Mall in Washington, as a great civic center.

In the older parts of cities, where real estate values are high, the creation of wide thoroughfares, where none were originally laid out, is an operation so costly that it is seldom undertaken, except under press of special circumstances; but sometimes it must be done, and it is mainly with a view to safeguarding the interests of the future where it can still be done at moderate expense that we shall urge New Haven to act in the matter of improving the present layout of thoroughfares. Yet there are two situations near the heart of the city that demand bold treatment at an early date: that of the serious and increasing congestion of traffic at Church and Chapel streets, and that of a proper approach to the city from the proposed new railroad station. The latter is pressing because the opportunity for securing it at moderate expense will soon pass away if not promptly grasped; the former because the inconvenience and delay seriously interfere with the business of the city.

The method which we propose for dealing with these two closely related situations is set forth at the beginning of the Specific Recommendations, page 47, but no general statement upon the subject of main thoroughfares can be intelligible without a brief discussion of the traffic conditions leading to the congestion at Church and Chapel streets. That congestion is due to the combination of several circumstances: first, the two street car lines, so situated that cars upon them are in greater demand than upon any other lines in the city, cross each other at grade, which reduces the capacity of each line more than half and inevitably causes congestion and delay; second, the necessary transfer of a great number of passengers at this crossing, where the present arrangements afford no waiting-room and no landing platform for these passengers, except the street immediately adjacent to the crossing; third, the natural route for ordinary street traffic from the railroad station, from the southern and southwestern parts of the city, and from the New York highway, to the northern and northeastern parts of the city and to the highway to Hartford and Boston, intersects the principal line of east and west street traffic at this very point of congestion in the local railway system.   To so arrange the streets of a town as to force a great stream of wagons and automobiles to travel over the platforms and through one end of the main waiting-room of an important railroad station, would be no more dangerous or inconvenient than the combination of transfer station and highways at Church and Chapel streets is fast becoming.

There are three principal highways for local and suburban passenger travel from the north: the State Street line, tapping the northeastern industrial district and the whole Quinnipiac Valley; the Whitney Avenue line, tapping the high-class northern residential district and the country north of Mill Rock and Lake Whitney; and the Dixwell Avenue line together with the Northampton Division of the New York, New Haven & Hartford Railroad, tapping the northwesterly part of the city and the large tract of country between Mill Rock and West Rock and to the north.   By electrifying the Northampton Division and diverting the outer part of the Dixwell Avenue traffic to it, by tunneling in Whitney Avenue from Trumbull Street, and by turning the State Street cars through Grove Street into the right-of-way, all the passenger traffic from the north can be brought together (below street grade) at the intersection of the Northampton Division with Whitney Avenue or Temple Street.   It seems reasonable to suppose that such a concentration can and will be brought about and a subway constructed from there to a point to the south of George Street, where the high ground falls away, where the southern and southwestern car lines begin to diverge and where there is no longer any heavy east and west traffic to be crossed. In one form or another such a separation of grades seems to be the only satisfactory escape from a transit situation that is rapidly becoming intolerable.   The specific method of dealing with this problem which we have to suggest is considered below (page 56).   No changes on the present surface, such as street widening, nor any re-routing of cars short of sending them to parts of the city where the passengers do not want to go, can radically relieve this central difficulty.

Apart from the solution of the problem presented by the central "knot" of street car congestion, New Haven has to face the fact that most of the main thoroughfares radiating from the city are not wide enough to carry conveniently and expeditiously the general traffic which is already, or is soon to be, thrown upon them.   Yet, if action is not too long delayed, much of the trouble can be remedied without extravagant expense, by taking advantage of the fact that, through the custom of setting buildings various distances back from the street, front dooryards have been left between the buildings and the edge of the sidewalk.   As traffic increases and the lots come to be used for business purposes, such dooryards become inconvenient and undesirable, and one by one the buildings are either extended to the sidewalk by new additions or new buildings are erected on the sidewalk line.   The reason for this change is not usually that additional lot depth is required, for often considerable yards are left unoccupied at the rear; but it is simply that on a commercial street the buildings need to be as close to the stream of traffic as possible, and, since the individual lot owner cannot move the street as a whole up to his building, he has to extend or move his building to the street.   His immediate purpose is thus served and ultimately the whole row of buildings is thus advanced to the street line in response to changed conditions.   But at just about the time that this process is fully completed, the volume of traffic flowing over the street is apt to have become so great that everybody recognizes the street to be too narrow for the increased traffic it has now to carry. If the case is a bad one, the inconvenience due to overcrowding the traveled way will in time reach a point where, in spite of the great cost of such an operation, the buildings along one or both sides of the street must be destroyed and new building lines must be established—it may be on the very lines where most of the original buildings stood before the increase in traffic offered inducements to move them forward to the sidewalk. Indeed, it may be said as a general rule that, on any street where the buildings are set back from the sidewalk line, (provided it is not a strictly local way without any general traffic and provided the lots are not exceptionally shallow) the very advancement of a few buildings to the sidewalk line is a sign which points directly to the growth of travel and indicates that ample width will soon be needed in that thoroughfare.

As soon as these conditions appear it is time to act. As we have said, it is not in most cases the desire to utilize a greater depth of lot which leads to the change, but the desire to get next the sidewalk and to do away with a front yard which has served its purpose and is not desired under the new conditions. If the street is one likely to have a considerable amount of through travel, it ought at once to be laid out wide enough to handle such travel, and the cost of the land taken for the widening ought to be charged up, at least in part, to the abutters, who get by the change,—what many of them already want and what the rest soon will want,—direct frontage on a busy sidewalk.

A still wiser course of procedure would be to lay out the main thoroughfares before any buildings have been advanced to the sidewalk line, and to make them wide enough between building lines to serve all probable future requirements; but to leave the sidewalk location unchanged until the growth of travel or the demands of the abutters call for shifting it over to the established building line. This is the invariable practice in Washington and in most well-conducted European cities. It is the plan to some extent in New York, where just recently the sidewalks of Fifth Avenue have been moved back against the building line on the space formerly occupied by stoops, areaways and dooryards. Sixteenth Street and Pennsylvania Avenue in Washington are both laid out 160 feet wide from building line to building line, but Sixteenth Street is a fine residence street without heavy traffic and with no commercial business, while Pennsylvania Avenue is an important business artery. On the latter the wide sidewalks are in immediate contact with the fronts of the buildings, as is proper for a business street, and the roadway with car tracks in the middle is more than wide enough to carry all the traffic that can ever be concentrated on it; whereas, on Sixteenth Street, the traveled portion of the street, including sidewalks and the space for sidewalk trees, is only 80 feet wide and all the houses have front dooryards 40 feet deep, which the householders are at liberty to fence and use almost as freely as if they owned them without encumbrance. At the same time all the householders are protected against the premature action of any individual lot owner, who might see a possible advantage in being among the first to bid for a commercial business by building a flat-house with stores under it out upon the sidewalk line 40 feet in advance of the other houses. The latter is the sort of thing that is happening every now and then in New Haven, on streets where the great majority of the owners would prefer to have the set-back continued for some years longer. In Washington this crowding forward cannot be done, but when a reasonably large proportion of the owners on any street, or any block of a street, are ready for the change, the front yards are abolished and the sidewalk is moved over into contact with the buildings. If a single owner wants to put in a store

No. 5. Street in Budapest in front of the museum, showing provision for various kinds of travel and for street trees as well.

long before his neighbors are ready to give up their front yards and long before the city is ready to widen the street for the sake of increasing its traffic capacity, he is of course at liberty to do so, but he must not move forward of the general building line.   What he usually does is to abolish his own front dooryard and substitute an extra wide piece of sidewalk paving in place of it, sometimes using the space for outdoor stands, or show cases to attract trade.   He may even be permitted to erect light temporary structures or awnings on the spaces between his main building and the present sidewalk line, under which in good weather he can do a very good business.

Now it is just as certain as anything human can be, that the main thoroughfares of New Haven will become very inconveniently crowded unless they are made wide enough, from curb to curb, to permit a wagon to pass between the electric cars in the middle of the street and wagons drawn up against the curb, or slowly moving along it.   That practical requirement fixes an abso-lute definite minimum, below which a street having any considerable amount of traffic is certain to be inconvenient and inadequate and to cause endless troubles and delays.   The least allow-ance between curbs which will give this minimum capacity for thoroughfares is about 50 feet, and collisions and locked wheels are apt to occur at that.   A greater clearance than 50 feet is desirable, even with cars and wagons and loads of the size now employed, while the tendency is certainly to increase the size and capacity of cars and other vehicles, especially of automobile trucks and vans.   Probably about 55 feet between curbs should be regarded as the minimum desirable width for important thoroughfares.*

For streets of moderate width it is customary, both in American and European cities, to allot for sidewalks about one-fifth of the total width: that is, to divide the street into the propor-tions 1: 3: 1.   For a 50-foot roadway this calls for sidewalks 16 2-3 feet wide, or for a 55-foot roadway sidewalks 18 1-3 feet wide.   A width of 15 or 20 feet is no more than reason-able for a business street, as anyone can see who will examine the crowded condition of the sidewalks in New Haven's business district during rush hours.   Thus a minimum width between building lines of 80 to 95 feet, for the main thoroughfares of New Haven, would sooner or later be profitably occupied for every inch of its surface, and in many cases a considerably greater width would in time prove desirable from the most utilitarian point of view.

If any attempt is to be made to keep trees on the main streets of the "City of Elms," more space than 83 feet is certainly needed, for sidewalks only 16 or 17 feet wide in front of continu-ous buildings are not proper places to grow trees.   Trees would encumber the sidewalk space, which is all needed for business, and trees growing within 15 feet of the buildings, especially where sidewalk vaults are constructed, are in no position to grow properly, even if trees so placed would not become a nuisance by blanketing the windows of the buildings.   A width of 100 feet or more between building lines for highways likely to become main thoroughfares is no more than a reasonable allowance and about 85 or 90 feet should be considered the normal minimum.

In this connection it is interesting to note the standard widths adopted in European cities. London† requires 48 feet between curbs and 80 feet between buildings for secondary avenues, 100 feet over all for principal arteries, and proposes 140 feet over all for two great main arteries which are being considered.   In German cities of the class to which New Haven

---

* In the report of the Metropolitan Improvement Commission of Massachusetts, 1909, this subject is discussed at length.   Fifty-four feet is considered insufficient and 60 feet recommended as desirable for six lines of vehicles, including street cars.

† English street cars are narrower than American cars.

belongs, such as Leipzig, Frankfort and Hanover, the standards are as follows: for strictly local streets, 33 to 47 feet; for secondary thoroughfares, 50 to 80 feet; and for main thoroughfares, 85 to 118 feet. A Prussian law in force since 1875, apparently drawn up with regard to the requirements of Berlin with its heavier traffic, lays down the following dimensions for the laying out of new streets and for the alteration of old ones: local streets, 40 to 65 feet; secondary thoroughfares, 65 to 95 feet; main thoroughfares, over 95 feet. But the figure of about 85 feet is really the most critical one from a practical point of view, as being the least which will allow a free gangway wide enough for a single row of vehicles between wagons drawn up at the curb and street cars moving on tracks in the middle of the street. And yet the highways plainly marked as the permanent main thoroughfares of New Haven seldom reach these figures. Many of them have some such width between buildings at present for the greater part of their length, but in general no steps have been taken to avoid the recurrence of the rapid contraction of the space by the advancement of buildings to the property line, that is to say, to the edge of the present traveled sidewalk, about the same time that the need of providing for increased travel begins to be apparent.

We earnestly recommend that the city take steps to establish forthwith new building lines along all such of its present and prospective main thoroughfares as are not yet generally built up to the existing street lines, and to prepare and adopt plans for the physical widening of these thoroughfares, with a view to putting them into effect only when demanded by the abutters or by the requirements of general traffic. In many instances where the contraction of the thoroughfares by the erection of more or less costly structures directly on the present street lines has already gone on to a considerable extent, it may be necessary to skip such expensive structures in the establishment of the new line and leave them undisturbed until the actual physical widening of the street at all points becomes urgent.

A method for dealing with this matter without running into excessive expense a long time in advance of actual necessity, while at the same time safeguarding the interests of the future, is suggested by methods occasionally employed in European cities. In the first place, let a definite plan for the ultimate widening of certain main thoroughfares be officially adopted as desirable,—as a thing to be worked toward by degrees. Second, let some regularly constituted municipal authority, such as the Board of Public Works, be granted a standing discretionary authority to extend the boundaries of any of these main thoroughfares to the proposed limits of widening, upon any lot or lots at any point within the plan at any time which may seem expedient, provided only that the estimated net damages due to such extension of the street limits within any calendar year shall not exceed a certain fixed sum appropriated as a contingent fund for meeting such damages. Third, let it be required that, before the issuance of any permit for building or rebuilding or important alteration upon property lying within the limits of the plan of proposed ultimate widening of any main thoroughfare, due notice must be given to the Board of Public Works (or other authority charged with the discretionary power above described), in order that action may be taken in due season in each case to prevent the erection of structures which would add needlessly to the cost of ultimate widening.

A process of gradual widening, as the various buildings along a street are from time to time torn down by their owners in order to replace them with new ones, is a not uncommon process in European cities. It is a very sensible and economical way of gradually bringing about results which everybody recognizes as desirable in the long run, but which would involve serious financial burdens if put through all at once. It may be objected that the patchwork appearance of the street *ad interim* is unsightly, with here and there a wide place where new buildings have gone up and alternating with them narrow parts which expose the blank side walls of old buildings projecting beyond the new ones.   Yet, in cities where the sense of civic beauty is far more acute than it generally is in America, this temporarily ragged condition is accepted as a small price to pay for the economical and certain accomplishment of a great permanent improvement.   In New Haven, indeed, the same ragged condition often occurs, but only as a process of narrowing, and the application of the principle to streets where the great majority of the houses are now set back from the street line, would prevent the occurrence of the very raggedness to which the system leads when applied to the widening of a street that is already closely built.   In our preliminary study of this problem we have noted some of the obvious lines of traffic for which provision is evidently insufficient.   These are indicated on the map and referred to later on in this report, more by way of illustration and example than as an attempt to offer conclusive advice. The matter is one for the proper and businesslike handling of which the city ought first to secure a carefully drawn enabling act, which will provide the necessary powers and machinery for designating the main thoroughfares and fixing the new limits thereof (after careful study and public hearings), for surveying and establishing the new lines, for ascertaining the damages and for assessing upon the abutters against the damages a fair share of the cost.

Since first drafting our report the question has been raised and called to our attention as to whether the city has the power to permit property owners to build cornices and projections over a street beyond the line of the street and whether the power should be exercised if it exists.

Without attempting to offer a legal opinion as to the powers of the City of New Haven in this respect, we can say that such powers have been generally exercised by other cities both in this country and in Europe.   It is customary, and is generally regarded as entirely within the legal discretion of city authorities, to permit such projections beyond the street line *as do not interfere with the use of the street.*   Under this heading it is almost universal to allow projections below the surface, such as sidewalk vaults; it is not uncommon (except on narrow streets and sidewalks) systematically to authorize moderate projections at and near the surface of the street, such as steps, area railings, and columns, mouldings, sculptural decorations, etc., about openings; it is not uncommon systematically to authorize projections, such as bay windows, containing usable space forming an integral part of a building, to be extended out over the street line at levels high enough not to interfere with travel in the street; it is almost universal to authorize (if not by special action at least by routine approval of the building department and by passive acquiescence) the erection of cornices, eaves and other such architectural features, projecting at a high level into the street from the wall of a building erected on the street line.

In many cities permits for various kinds of projections are systematically issued.   In some cases a fee is collected by the city on the issuance of such a permit, in some cases an annual fee is charged, and in some cases the city receives no compensation.   In some cities the issuance of such a permit for a cash consideration has been declared illegal.   In most cases we believe the license to the abutter to maintain such a projection is at least in theory revocable, in case the city decides that conditions have so changed that the projection interferes with the proper use of the street.   It is only upon the theory that it did not so interfere at the time it was authorized that its permission could be legally supported.   We believe there are decisions sustaining the prescriptive right of abutters to the continued use of sidewalk vaults, even when the city authorities have decided that they need the space for public purposes, and there may be such decisions in regard to projections above the ground level; but we understand that in the Fifth Avenue cases the courts have sustained the contention of the City of New York that projection above the surface of the sidewalk, although originally erected with the full approval of the city, must be removed without compensation to the owners whenever the city government decides that the needs of traffic demand the space they occupy.

The above general statement, made without looking up specific cases for citation, may throw some light upon the question of whether the city has the power to permit property owners to erect projections beyond the street line.

The expediency of exercising such a power turns upon a large group of circumstances, of which the most important are: the width of the streets, the amount of present and prospective traffic, and the height of the buildings, as determined either by law or by custom and economic conditions. It is hardly necessary to point out that with streets as wide as those of Washington and with the height of buildings regulated by law as it is in that city, to say nothing of the hotter sun and greater need of shade, there is much less objection to permitting large projecting cornices and more excuse for doing so than on the narrow downtown streets of the financial districts of New York or Boston. New Haven occupies an intermediate position, but a considerable portion of its streets are narrower than is desirable and projections upon their limited space should be jealously watched.

There are, however, distinct objections to the policy of always drawing a sharp line between the private property and the street and saying to the abutter: "You may build solidly up to this line but you may not build an inch farther for any purpose whatever. If you want to provide for cornices and columns and decorative architectural projections, you must set your main wall back far enough behind that of your neighbors to allow for such luxuries." Such a policy simply puts a premium upon a commercialized monotony of unrelieved walls, perforated with holes serving as doors and windows.

It is very desirable that there should be a zone into which the main walls of the buildings should not be allowed to encroach, but in which architectural ornament and other desirable projections may be permitted and encouraged. From the point of view of practical results, it is immaterial whether the legal *status* of this zone is that of private property subject to restrictions against occupation for building purposes except by the authorized and limited projections, or whether it is legally a part of the street into which such projections are permitted to extend.

On the whole, because of the legal and administrative difficulties connected with applying and maintaining in perpetuity special and varied restrictions on private property, and because of the liability that conditions may arise calling for changes in the use of the intermediate zone, it is generally a better public policy to make this zone a part of the street and under full public control. But of course it is a corollary of the latter method that the street lines should include a correspondingly greater width. When streets are relatively narrow and it is impracticable either to widen them or to secure a partially restricted zone upon the adjacent private property, it is probably best to adopt regulations similar to those generally applicable in Paris, which permit no projection beyond the street line at the street level or within a certain distance above it (equivalent to the height of a low first story); which permit certain limited projections above that level (the maximum projection being fixed in relation to the width of the street); and which, finally, fix a building height limitation also dependent upon the width of the street.

Street Trees, Poles and Wires, Advertising Signs.

Regardless of any natural pride that New Haven might have in justifying her name as the "City of Elms," there is urgent need of action if the street trees are not to fall below the standard even of the average careless American town.   In the business district there are few if any streets sufficiently wide to justify the attempt to maintain trees permanently there; such trees as now exist can be doctored and cared for until they must be removed, but any attempt at replanting would in most cases prove not only very costly, but also futile.   The growing business district has crowded, abused and neglected the trees, until they are now in a pitiable condition at best, and many may better be removed at once than be allowed to die gradually. Upon streets beyond the more crowded business district and upon the public open spaces, notably the Green, New Haven is fairly well provided with shade and ornamental trees, but even there the conditions are fast changing, due to severe attacks of disease and insects which the half-starved trees are not able properly to resist.   The need for immediate care and considerable

No. 6.   View of the Green as it appeared when the Elms were at their best.

expenditure is everywhere evident, and only by such care will it be possible to maintain New Haven's reputation for noble shade trees, which appears to be due, rather to the foresight of individuals many years ago and to the accidental occurrence in the past of conditions favorable to their growth, than to any systematic care in recent years. Where in many cases there are reasons for removing trees, this work is seldom done with any system, or after any serious consideration as to whether the time has come when trees can no longer be wisely maintained in a given street. Again, in many cases the trees are not deliberately removed by anybody, even one by one, but simply die through neglect. They are in some places standing so close together that, as they grow older and become crowded, the foliage of the individual trees has insufficient exposure to the light and the vitality of the trees is seriously lowered. Again, the covering of the roots with impervious pavements has changed, greatly for the worse, the conditions under which the trees attained their present growth. The presence of more or less smoke and gas in the air, the reflection of the hot summer sun from the neighboring walls and pavements, and a hundred other conditions that inevitably accompany the city's growth, are all tending to lower the vitality òf the trees and render them less capable of withstanding the attacks of insects, diseases and wounds.

One of New Haven's assets as a pleasant place to live in is the comeliness of its shade trees. On any reasonable basis of valuation, tree for tree, it has a large amount of capital so invested. It is not a negotiable asset, for the trees as so much standing lumber would fetch but a trifling fraction of their actual value as shade trees; but it is none the less a valuable asset and one which can be to a great extent preserved and increased, or which can by neglect be completely lost.

The value of street trees is frequently placed very high in damage suits, and even on the most moderate basis mounts up to a large total for the entire city. In the city of Hartford a detailed inventory of street trees has been taken. The valuation placed on the individual trees, although of necessity somewhat arbitrary, is generally accepted by the interested abutters as fair. A perfect specimen of the best species of trees, properly placed and free from disease or injury, with a trunk having a cross section area of one square foot, is reckoned as worth $75.00, but the average street tree scales down much below this value in the inventory. On any residence street lined by rows of beautiful, large, healthy trees, one to every 50-foot lot, it would be hard to find any abutter who would be ready to accept $75.00 as adequate personal compensation if a telephone company, for example, should propose to cut down all the trees in the street; and it would be difficult to win the consent of most of the abutters to such a devastation even for a much larger cash consideration. This method of looking at the subject perhaps gives as fair an idea of the real value to the abutters of well-grown street trees as can easily be got, and it suggests that the Hartford method of valuing trees is probably conservative. We have figures covering about three-quarters of that city, prepared on the basis above described, and the total value of the public investment in street trees in that area reaches the sum of about $450,000.00.

We cite this instance because few people realize that the shade tree business, if the city is going into it at all, is a big and serious business and that, if adequate returns are to be secured on the investment, the business must be handled in a businesslike way and with a reasonable and proportionate relation between the annual expenditure for protection, maintenance, renewal, etc., and the total value of the result aimed at. If, on the other hand, the city should decide that it does not want or cannot afford anything better than ragged rows of crowded trees, gradually starving and dying off before they reach their prime through lack of adequate food, water and air, and through untreated injuries to their bark, limbs and foliage, it may reasonably let the matter go along in the usual half-hearted way with the usual results.

The town of Brookline has a Street Tree Committee and appropriates annually a few thousand dollars for planting and maintenance, in addition to the fund for gypsy moth extermination.   This maintenance fund amounts to about 25 cents per tree, or $77.00 for each mile of street under consideration.   Under the committee new trees are set and properly watered in the summer, old trees are doctored or removed, and the responsibility is thus definitely placed where it may be attended to.

Some systematic planting on the newer streets is desirable; but the crying needs of the street trees are: first, systematic and thorough protection from insect attacks, by spraying and otherwise; second, the removal of superfluous trees before they so reduce the vitality of their betters as to open the way for disease and degeneration; third, some systematic protection against the barking of the trunks by horses and otherwise, and against rot entering through dead limbs and other mechanical injuries; and finally, in many cases, provision for ventilating, feeding and watering at the roots when pavements are laid.

While the street trees, still the most beautiful feature of New Haven streets, are becoming an almost irreparable loss through their rapid deterioration, the next most obvious positive injury to the appearance of the city is the defacement due to overhead wires, street poles and advertising

No. 7.   Chapel Street in 1865, before the days of wires and before the tall buildings and crowded car tracks
proved the streets to be too narrow.

signs.   Mr. F. L. Ford, city engineer of Hartford, in writing on this subject says: "Overhead wires in a city are always objectionable.   They are dangerous because of liability to fall during any storm, particularly ice-storms.   During fires they not only hinder the work of the firemen,

No. 8.   Church Street as it is now, choked with overhead wires, taken up by cars and made hideous by an incongruous jumble of signs.

but are often a menace to their lives. All wires are in the way because, though not in themselves dangerous, they are liable to become so by crossing with others which are, and must be handled as if heavily charged. They damage shade trees, which have to be cut to avoid any wires on the street, and if the wires are numerous the shape of the trees is often ruined.   They injure the appearance of any street or yard where they are strung.   A further damage, as compared with underground cables, arises from the loss of service which ensues when overhead wires are broken by storms or cut by

fire.   The public pays for continuous service, and comes nearer to securing it if all wires are underground.   All damage increases rapidly with the number of wires, and is the greatest on the narrowest and busiest streets." New Haven has overhead wires, and the city, with the aid of a competent disinterested expert, should enter into conference with the public service corporations operating the wires, and should then determine upon a definite policy in regard to the removal of overhead wires, should fix a fair and reasonable rate of progress for the work of putting them underground, and should then insist rigorously upon the advancement of the work

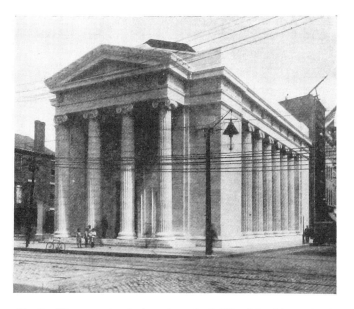

No. 9.   The new savings bank, an interesting building defaced by overhead wires.

at the rate specified.   Beginning in the central districts and working outward, the removal should apply at once to all overhead wires in the streets, with the exception of the trolley wires and span wires of the electric roads.

In the more crowded thoroughfares it is seriously worth considering whether it would not be worth while to adopt a practice that is becoming very general in the downtown streets of

European cities, and in Portland, Oregon, in this country—that of attaching the trolley span wires directly to the walls of the abutting buildings and thus getting rid of poles altogether and having perfectly free clear sidewalks.   In such cases the street lights are generally suspended also from span wires over the middle of the street, or from brackets attached to the buildings.   Not only is every inch of space in the street thus made available for traffic, but the appearance is made surprisingly spacious, clean and orderly.

Extravagant advertising signs and billboards greatly injure the aspect of many New Haven streets.   No one can question that the presence of large and frequently garish advertising signs, designed specifically to stand out strikingly from their surroundings and violently arrest the attention, is more or less irritating and annoying to most people and tends to make the city less agreeable in appearance.   Not infrequently an acceptable piece of information is conveyed to the mind, especially in the case of posters announcing some entertainment or other passing event, but it is very seldom that the ordinary citizen gets any advantage from the signs and posters that begins to compensate him for the annoyance.   It is clearly a case where the privilege of the abutter upon a public highway to see and be seen by the passing throng is liable to abuse, and frequently is abused to the detriment of the general public which pays for maintaining the street.   When the abuse goes so far as to give indubitable offence to public morals or health through the nature of the advertisement, or through the erection of a shield which invites the commission of nuisances by others, or when the abuse goes so far as to cause serious risk of life, limb or property through the maintenance of structurally dangerous or inflammable billboards, then the courts will protect a claimant under the law of nuisance, if anybody is willing to take the trouble to go to law about a matter which is everybody's business and therefore nobody's business.   In our easy-going American way most of us hate to take an unpleasant initiative, or to risk getting the reputation of being fault-finding busybodies; so we do not get the relief and protection from such nuisances which we might get even under the common law.   And since the courts are somewhat ultra-conservative and cautious about interfering arbitrarily with an individual's use of his own property, the abuse has to be a crying and outrageous one before they will order it to be abated under the law of nuisance. Up to that point there is now, therefore, no legal relief or mitigation of the abuse.

The most effective way to deal with the billboard nuisance then appears to be by license and taxation,—the same method that is used to control many other business enterprises which are legitimate but liable to abuse.   The requirement of a license before any sign may be publicly exhibited, other than one relating to business carried on upon the premises; the requirement that any sign, or structure for the support and exhibition of signs or posters, which may be erected under the license, shall be securely built and of fireproof material, and that the design shall be approved by the licensing authority; the imposition of a reasonably heavy annual license tax based upon the size of the sign or billboard authorized by the license; and a proviso that the license may be revoked or suspended at the discretion of the licensing authority in case any immoral, indecent or fraudulent advertisement is exhibited—these measures are legally practicable and will tend to keep the abuses of the business within bounds.

The Sewerage Problem.

The system of sewerage which has been followed in New Haven in the past, and which is now being followed, is one in which the storm water from the streets and other surfaces is turned into the sewers that carry the house sewage into the harbor.   But because these sewers have to run such long and constantly increasing distances, the cost of making them large enough to carry all the storm water falling upon the whole extent of the city would be very great, and they are now by no means able to carry it. Instead of this they overflow at every heavy rainstorm into the nearest natural brook or river channel, filling it with rain water mixed with street sweepings and diluted sewage. From time to time, as this discharge begins to cause a serious nuisance at any point, a covered channel or storm sewer must be built to take the over-flow from the regular sewer and carry the offensive matter a little further on. Thus the nuisance at Beaver Ponds will soon be transferred to or toward West River by the construction of such a storm sewer. Now, the West River looks like a good-sized stream, and it has a fairly broad channel for the three miles between the mouth of Beaver Brook and the harbor, but so much of the head waters have been impounded by the New Haven Water Company that its ordinary fresh water flow is very small, and even if it had the full discharge from its watershed, the cur-rent in all the upper part of the tidal portion would be slight. Under these circumstances, with the growth of population in New Haven during the next two or three generations, and the conse-quent increase in pollution, the discharge of diluted sewage from the storm overflows along its banks and those of its tributaries, will tend to convert West River into one long, open, reeking cesspool. Boston has spent over two million dollars in building a channel for Stony Brook, big enough to carry the heavy storm floods of spring and covered up tight enough to conceal and carry away secretly the more heavily contaminated summer flow. A covered channel big enough to carry the West River, or even big enough to intercept and carry off to the harbor all the storm water that will flow from the sewered area on the watershed of the West River, fifty years from now, would be a huge undertaking.

For a small area the combined system of sewerage—one pipe for both house sewage and storm water—is much the simplest and cheapest; but, as the area to be dealt with gets bigger and constantly bigger, the time generally comes, sooner or later, when a double or "separate" system is undeniably cheaper and better, permitting the clean storm water to be turned into the nearest open brooks or channels, while the much more limited and constant volume of foul sewage is piped, regardless of wet or dry season, to points where it can be disposed of without serious nuisance or danger. The city of New Haven has outgrown conditions favorable to combined sewers, and the longer it postpones the evil day of facing the need of a changed system, the more serious the difficulties and the greater the expense involved will be. It would probably be impos-sible to calculate how many million dollars it has cost Boston to postpone as long as she did the adoption of the policy of a separate storm sewer system, but the cost and the unfortunate results of the delay have been enormous. Recognizing these conditions, we feel bound to call attention to the desirability of a thorough, farsighted, scientific study of the sewerage problem of New Haven as one important means toward city improvement. We do not pretend to have made an expert study of these matters and it is possible that New Haven is now proceeding along the path of wisdom and economy in the design and construction of its sewers; but the experience of other cities seems to give warning that it is at least time to investigate the situation and to see just to what the present routine is leading.

Local Parks and Playgrounds.

In considering the most profitable distribution of lands to be reserved for park purposes it is necessary to bear in mind two distinct methods of use: frequent use by the immediate neigh-bors as a local park, and general use by a large number of persons who make infrequent visits and do not depend upon the park in question for almost daily exercise. It frequently happens that a park may be so developed as to serve for both local and general uses, but, if a park system is to be secured that will meet the legitimate public demands for both purposes, it is necessary to consider the two separately and to make sure that proper provision is made for each purpose. The local use of parks and recreation grounds is by people within easy walking distance of them. If the people of the city, if in particular the women and children, are to have the benefit of a place where they may habitually get a little healthful recreation out of doors under agreeable and refreshing surroundings, as a part of the ordinary routine of life; if the children are to be able to make such use of a playground; if their elders are to get with tolerable frequency even a little walk in a park or square for air and for refreshment from the dulling routine of life in factory, store, office, and cramped dwelling house or flat; if the mothers are to get out occasionally to a pleasant park bench with their sewing or what not, while the children play about them: then facilities for this sort of recreation must be provided within *easy walking distance* of every home in the city. Any plan that deliberately stops short of such provision and leaves any considerable neighborhoods permanently without the benefit of accessible parks and playgrounds for local use, while providing other districts with such facilities at the general expense, is in so far illogical, unjust, undemocratic and unwise. We may say, then, that in a reasonably well-planned city there should be, within easy reach of every family of citizens, local or neighborhood grounds; places for active games and exercises, for public concerts and other similar passive pleasures, and for the enjoyment of spaciousness, of refreshing beauty, of the freshness of verdure and especially of airiness, in so far as such enjoyment may be attainable under the controlling conditions. The size of such grounds may vary greatly, and the size should influence the frequency and distribution; so, too, the special purposes subserved by each open space must vary—ranging from the simple possibilities of the little squares and the grounds of schools and other public buildings, and from the limited uses of specially equipped grounds, such as athletic grounds, public bath houses and recreation piers, to the many varieties of recreation which may be provided for upon the large and complex local parks. The real value of local grounds often depends as much upon skillful treatment as upon size; a space may be made to serve only one or two purposes, or it may be made to serve many; so, too, it may be made to provide for but few people, or it may be made to provide effectively for many. It often happens that much value is lost through the attempt to use a single piece of ground for two or more practically incompatible purposes.

Just how great an area is needed for local grounds in any section of the city, is difficult to determine; the extent is greatly affected by the varying efficiency of the design and management of the grounds themselves, and is further affected by the density and character of the urban population in that section. The city of Chicago* is now proceeding upon the principle that no dwelling should be *more* than half a mile from grounds adapted to serve the local purposes. The population within a radius of half a mile is normally great enough to require, and to use to its full capacity, park area quite as large as can ordinarily be set apart in a single piece without interrupting important streets, and greater distance offers a serious obstacle to the easy and habitual use of such grounds by women and children. Indeed, since mothers and babies in need of recreation grounds and young boys and girls in want of playgrounds cannot be induced to walk more than a very short distance, such neighborhood grounds ought if possible to be brought within a quarter of a mile of every dwelling.

* Report of the Special Park Commission upon a Metropolitan Park System, December, 1904.

It is the conclusion of the South Park Commissioners of Chicago, based upon their experience with the most complete series of well-equipped neighborhood recreation grounds that has yet been established in any city, that a unit of less than about twenty acres in extent gives far less valuable returns in public usefulness, compared with its annual cost, than a unit of that size or over.

If each 20-acre park be reckoned to serve a district of one square mile of city, which would mean a rather longer walk from the outskirts of the park than is desirable, the park would occupy 3.1 per cent. of the total area. Making due allowance for a reasonable distribution of little squares and triangles, in addition to the main neighborhood playground and park area, these figures would seem to suggest that about 5 per cent. of the total area devoted to local park purposes is as little as can be considered a fair provision. If, instead of one square mile of city, the district served adequately by a local park of 20 acres be assumed as that within a quarter of a mile in a straight line from the nearest part of the park, the percentage is increased. In the case of square parks of 20 acres, the park would occupy 7.7 per cent. of each district, which would mean a minimum allowance of not less than 8 to 10 per cent. of the city area devoted to parks and squares.

Any estimate on the basis of 5 per cent. of the area devoted to parks would certainly have to be increased in the case of an abnormally dense urban population, in order to provide space to accommodate the crowds, quite apart from the question of proximity.

The accompanying map of the city (No. 10) shows existing park and playground areas, but does not show the schoolyards, which are so small that they cannot be shown on this scale and are as a rule utterly inadequate for playground purposes. Around the parks, squares and playgrounds, regardless of the character of each, are shown zones of influence, representing the areas which can be said to have the minimum normal provision of local park space, an inner zone shown in white extending one-quarter mile from the nearest corner of the park, and an outer shaded zone between one-quarter and one-half mile from the park. In some cases these zones have been arbitrarily curtailed, because the park or square is so small that it cannot be expected to serve so large an area; and in no case, therefore, is the zone of influence of a park shown as extending to cover an area more than twenty times as large as the park itself, that is to say, an area of which the park comprises 5 per cent., the minimum above discussed. The white zones may be considered to represent the proportion of the city which is well provided with parks for local purposes. The shaded zones may be considered to represent the proportion of the city lying more or less within the normal effective range of local parks—regions whose needs are not fully met, but which are better provided for than are the tracts shown in black. The black sections are those which lie too far removed from any park or playground to receive any practical benefit therefrom in the daily routine of its people. The diagram is but a graphical illustration of areas and distances as they now exist, and cannot be made to show the relation of the parks and squares to the distribution of the population. In all those territories shown in black additional facilities should be sought for playgrounds and for local parks.

With the exception of certain special sites, mentioned in the following pages, which have peculiar advantages for certain park purposes, the chief points to be considered in selecting land for local parks are cheapness and accessibility to the people who will use them. The best method of acquisition is, first, to decide upon the general locality within which the local park is needed, to examine carefully the assessed valuations of property within the locality, and to select (tentatively) one or more sites which seem promising as to location and cheapness. Then, second,

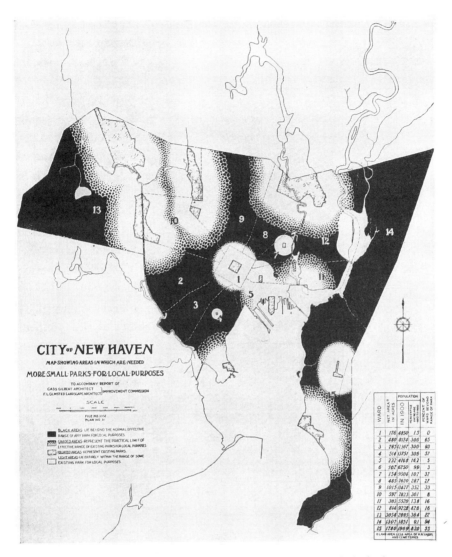

No. 10. Map showing in black areas in which are needed more small parks for local purposes.

to obtain options on such of the lands within the limits of the tentative site or sites as can be put under favorable options. The third step is to ask publicly for the tender of lands for park purposes in the locality under consideration and to hold public hearings thereon. And the final step is, in the light of all the information thus secured, to select definitely the site and boundaries of the park or playground and take all the land by condemnation proceedings. The land taken will ordinarily consist in whole or in part of tracts upon which options or public tenders of sale have been obtained at reasonable prices, and for such lands immediate settlement can be made at the price agreed upon; the price of other lots required to secure proper boundaries will be determined under condemnation proceedings, either by agreement or otherwise. It is far better to proceed in this way than to begin by purchasing or accepting certain pieces of land, no matter how favorable the terms may be, and subsequently acquiring adjacent pieces for the rectification of boundaries or completion of the requisite area; because the very establishment of a park renders the adjacent land more valuable at once, and if the city buys park land piecemeal, it has to pay in the later purchases an increased price, due simply to its

No. 11. Old garden at the Bristol house, built in 1800, recently destroyed for the Ives Memorial Library.

having previously started to establish a park in the neighborhood. The condemnation process, preceded by obtaining options where possible, takes all the land at one and the same instant and at the value of land in a district which has no parks.

Of course the regions where there is most pressing need of acquiring public recreation grounds, where the population is most dense and most rapidly increasing, are precisely the places where vacant land in any considerable blocks is not to be had. Although there are as yet few areas of much extent in New Haven, which do not contain a large proportion of vacant land or land which is put to very trifling productive use, such land is nevertheless scattered in small parcels and a great deal of it consists of the back ends of deep lots. Blocks vary much in size in New Haven and lots in the same neighborhood sometimes vary from 60 to 200 feet or more in depth. In a suburb where the people are fairly well-to-do and land is cheap, a lot 150 or 200 feet deep or more may be a sensible thing. In Fair Haven (Ward 12) deep lots may be seen where the houses do not occupy more than about 8 or 10 per cent. of the lot

No. 12. Interior of big block in pleasant semi-suburban condition still retained as gardens for the surrounding houses.

and the remainder is put to excellent use with garden, orchard and lawn. Again, in the blocks as far downtown and of as high value as those on the Elm Street side of the Green, the gardenlike backyards are used and enjoyed in a manner to justify their existence. But with the demands of the greater population, especially in the industrial districts, such lots become an economic misfit, and not only are they wasteful of land, but they lead directly to positive evils. Back tenements, unsanitary shacks, crowding, secrecy and filth are the results of crowding poor and ignorant people into a region where each of the insufficient number of dwellings has a long piece of waste land tucked in behind it out of sight. The dwellings are terribly needed, are more in demand in such a district than anything else except food, and the back tenement or lodging shack is the natural response of people who have waste land on their hands in a district where so few can afford to waste. But the ordinary back tenement itself is a frightfully wasteful method of

No. 13.   Interior of big block showing how it is beginning to be occupied by rear tenements unsanitary and in other ways objectionable.

No. 14.   Interior of big block showing three rear tenements which are crowded into the back area, improperly lighted and difficult to police.

housing, morally and socially as well as economically. In a district where the needs of the people cry out for cheap housing and for the greatest possible utilization of the land, where it is obvious that a good solution of the problem presented by the excessively deep lot cannot be reached by the individual lot owner, it becomes the duty of the city to step in and take a directing hand in the matter. One solution, where size and shape permit, would be to cut through a new street and open the back land to a better class of development. Another would be to acquire the interior land and form a block playground, clean, open, well lighted and policed.

Consider for a moment the waste of land in deep lots for city dwellings, taking a comparatively open standard of urban development such as has prevailed in New Haven in the past.

A given tract of land half a mile square, provided with streets occupying a third of the total area, will subdivide in 619 lots of the standard size of 50 x 150 feet. In such a district, when

No. 15. Present playgrounds of the future citizens.

the lots are all occupied, there will be no playgrounds for the children except the streets and the back yards; there will be no parks or squares or other open ground whatever. If, on the same tract with the same area in streets, the same number of houses should be erected on lots 50 x 125 feet in size, there would be left over 17.7 acres for purposes of public recreation. This would be more than enough, if well arranged, to assure for all time that every boy and young man, who will ever live in that district, shall have opportunity and inducement near his own home to play

baseball and all the other vigorous outdoor games that make for a sound body, a clean mind and a healthy nervous system; to provide space that could be set apart for a swimming pool to be put in operation whenever the neighborhood or the city might feel disposed to pay for constructing it and supplying the water; to provide that the little children could have a shallow pool for their own, with a clean sandy beach and bottom where they could wade and play with toy boats and make sand pies and forts as well as if they were to be taken to the ocean beach itself; and to

No. 16. Present playgrounds of the future citizens.

assure that for all time the dwellers in that district would have only to walk two or three blocks or so to find a pleasant open spot with shady paths and benches for summer use. No sane man can doubt the advantage of such a method of subdivision, with its slightly smaller lots supplemented by public parks.

Closely related to the public playground for local purposes, is the play space about the public schools. Provision for this in New Haven up to the present time has apparently been almost wholly ignored, as indicated by the table on the next page, which shows that the children, instead of having a provision of 30 or 40 square feet of space each in which to play, are in some cases crowded beyond all reason, merely dumped out and herded between classes or scattered after school.

Rural Parks and Reservations.

In East Rock and West Rock, New Haven has already obtained control of two comparatively large rural parks, having extreme picturesqueness and remarkable geological formation.

No. 17. Buildings where an open schoolyard should be.

In addition to these and to the two smaller valley parks of Beaver Pond and Edgewood, we are led to recommend that certain other areas be obtained before the encroachment of the city shall have destroyed their charm or increased too greatly the cost of acquiring them.

One of the striking features of the situation about New Haven is the large extent of lands held in connection with the waterworks. The New Haven Water Company, in pursuance of its duties as agent of the community for gathering, storing and supplying water, has acquired a series of great reservations for the protection of the water supply. These reservations must be kept substantially unoccupied and free from buildings so long as the water supply continues

TABLE OF PARKS IN NEW HAVEN IN 1909

Park	Area in acres	Ward	Remarks
New Haven Green	16.5	1	
Open space	.36	2	
Open space	.06	3	
Bay View Park	23.39	4	
Trowbridge Square	.80	4	
Waterside Park	17.51	5	
Wooster Square	4.66	6	
Jocelyn Square	3.14	7	
East Rock Park	43.34	8	
	96.21	12	
	242.13		In Town of Hamden
Beaver Ponds Park	106.65	9	
Edgewood Park	113.59	10	
Quinnipiac Park	10.78	11	Part in water now
West Rock Park	215.30	13	Very small portion in Woodbridge
Fort Hale Park	48.98	15	
Fort Wooster Park	17.02	15	
Clinton Park	8.07	12	
	967.69		

Note: A number of these areas are small tracts which are properly local parks or playgrounds.

PROVISION OF SCHOOLYARDS IN 1907.

Ward	NAMES OF SCHOOLS	Square Feet of Yard Area	Number of Children in Ward	Square Feet of Yard* per Child
1		11,500	1,174	10
2	Webster Scranton Street	31,000	2,172	14
3	Davenport Avenue West Street Cedar Street Hallock Street Welch Zunder	35,100	4,101	9
4	Day School Washington Greenwich Avenue Kimberly Avenue	32,700	4,028	8
5	Wooster Fair Street Whiting	21,800	1,190	18
6	Eaton Hamilton	18,000	1,710	10
7	Skinner	15,000	2,962	5
8	Humphrey Street Lovell W. Hooker Edwards Street	21,800	2,013	11
9	Winchester Shelton Avenue Dixwell Avenue	21,000	3,379	6
10	Dwight Street Roger Sherman Orchard Street	16,000	1,877	9
11	Woolsey Lloyd Street	11,000	1,579	7
12	Ezekiel Cheever Ferry Street Strong	17,200	2,776	6
13	No record		685	
14	Lenox Street Quinnipiac	22,000	512	44
15	Woodward Morris Cove	29,000	588	49

Note: This table is not quite accurate as complete statistics could not be obtained.

* For the schools in crowded London, 30 square feet per capita of *playground* space exclusive of other portions of schoolyard is regarded as the minimum acceptable allowance. In New Haven the space ought to be much more liberal.

to be taken from their catchment areas. They include a great variety of interesting scenery and some of them are already put to excellent use for purposes of recreation, as for example, the shores of Lake Whitney. The landscape of Lake Whitney is as much enjoyed by those who pass along the adjacent roads as that of any park lake could be, and upon one side its shores are in actual use for recreation by the Country Club.

Ordinarily where the agent of the community, in securing and managing its water supply is the municipal government, or other strictly public corporation, it is customary for the margins of reservoirs and for lands acquired to protect the sources of supply to be used freely for purposes of public recreation. Not infrequently large sums are spent in constructing roads, paths and fences, in establishing plantations and in maintaining and policing, in order to provide for the effective use of such lands for purposes of recreation, when there would be no justification for such expense if the business of water supply alone were regarded. The economic justification for such expenditures lies in the fact that they enable the public to get a valuable by-product in the way of public recreation out of property held for other purposes.

Where a community relies upon private enterprise to supply its water and offers to the investors in the water company as their only compensation cash payments proportioned to the quantity of water delivered, with the single definite demand that the quality and quantity of the water be maintained at a satisfactory standard, there is little or no inducement to spend the investors' money in developing a by-product of public recreation as a gratuity to the community, no matter how much value of this sort might be secured for a small additional outlay. That under such circumstances anything at all is spent, with a view to developing the recreative value of the waterworks properties, is due partly to sheer generosity and public spirit on the part of the company, and partly, we suppose, to a farsighted recognition of the fact that the public is largely ruled by sentiment in dealing with public service corporations, and that a reputation for regarding the general public interest and welfare as well as the size of dividends is one of the most valuable assets such a company can possess.

Beyond a certain point such a company cannot afford to go, and certainly ought not to be asked to go, in making investments that bring no cash returns, no matter how largely they might benefit the public in proportion to the size of the extra investment. Yet, considered as a permanent arrangement, or even one expected to endure for a century or two, it seems an absurd waste that thousands of acres of watershed reserve should stand practically idle, fenced in from the public, when a moderate expenditure for improvements, policing and maintenance would serve to make them available for public use and would relieve the city of the necessity, which will otherwise sooner or later be forced upon it, of purchasing and holding open for park purposes separate and independent tracts of land of a closely similar sort. Indeed, such a policy would be so absurdly wasteful that, sooner or later, some coöperative action is almost certain to be brought about through force of public opinion, by which the public shall realize upon the recreative value of the water holdings. This might be brought about as an incident of the purchase of the water company by the city, as has happened with so many cities that started with privately owned waterworks, or it might be brought about through some more complicated arrangement by which the city should take over those lands of the water company that are valuable for park purposes, and use them as parks, subject to such restrictions as may be necessary to protect the primary uses for which the lands were originally acquired.

Anyone who will tramp over the great estates lying within the area of the watersheds which are or should be controlled by the New Haven Water Company as a protection for their water supply, or who will even study their distribution on the map, cannot but recognize that the public of the next generation will be deeply concerned with the full utilization and the ultimate destiny of these important tracts of suburban land, which are so situated that the gradual development of the trolley system will soon make them readily accessible from all parts of the city.

It is a matter for serious and farsighted study and fair-minded negotiation, by the ablest and broadest men who can be secured to represent the city and the water company, to devise a wise, just and businesslike permanent policy for the control and development of these lands and for governing the relations of the city and the company in regard to them.

To give but one specific indication of the desirability of proceeding at once to the development of some such farsighted policy, we will instance the case of the holdings around Lake Saltonstall. Here is a great tract of land surrounding the lake, which must be controlled in order to preserve from contamination the rain water which flows into the lake and through it into the homes of New Haven. So long as this source of supply continues to be used, so long will the land have to be kept substantially in its present condition of woodland and pasture and field. Vast in area, containing unusually fine scenery, it lies only four miles from New Haven Green, and, with the development of trolleys and good roads accompanying the gradual occupation of more and more of the intervening open tracts by the spread of suburban development, its value as a permanent preserve of such scenery on a large scale, free for the enjoyment of all who are able to wander half a mile or so from a trolley, as well as those who can afford the costly pleasures of carriage or automobile, will constantly become greater. Considered merely as a source of water supply and looking many, many years into the future, the time would probably come when parts of this land would attain such value, and the whole of its water supply would have become so small a fraction of the total required for the city, that the value of the watershed for residential development might outweigh its value as a collecting reservoir.

It is inconceivable, however, judging from the experience of all large cities the world over, that its value to the public for purposes of recreation, when combined with that for water supply, would ever fall below its market value as private real estate. There may be plenty of time in which to bring about a combination of the park and water interests by some joint or unified control; there may be no hurry so far as concerns the actual watershed under the control of the water company; that company may even be proceeding in its forestry work and other management of the property so as to be developing the highest possible scenic value on the land; but if this tract is to be regarded as a permanent preserve of scenery as well as a water preserve, the most desirable boundaries will not be found to coincide precisely with those which limit the watershed. The crest of the remarkable rocky rampart which encloses the lake upon the west and northwest, marks the edge of the watershed; but, if a pleasure drive were built along this rampart—as it will be some day—its value would depend in no small measure upon the control of the narrow verge of level ground beside it and of the steep wooded slope below it to the westward. This land has now practically no market value except for the growing of cordwood or the quarrying of trap rock. It is in part owned by the water company. But the water company probably has no especial reason or excuse for wanting to burden itself with this extra strip of woodland. Neither has the city any good excuse for acquiring it, *unless as a part of an accepted policy* by which the adjacent land of the water company shall be certainly and permanently maintained as a scenic preserve. In pursuance of such a policy, the acquisition by the city of such fragments of land required to complete the boundaries of the water company's holdings in such a manner as to make them ultimately and fully available for public enjoyment would be a most profitable public investment in proportion to the amount of capital embarked upon it.

Apart from the water reserves, we have to suggest a considerable number of desirable park sites, the reasons for selecting which are set forth *seriatim* in the section of this report dealing with Specific Recommendations and Suggestions.

Parkways.

Because of the fact that large parks and reservations must be limited in number and must be comparatively remote from the major part of the citizens, and because they can usually be most economically situated in localities that are not traversed by important thoroughfares, it has been found that their usefulness is greatly enhanced by long narrow arms reaching out into the surrounding territory and forming parklike approaches, which in effect bring the parks much nearer to the citizens without seriously encroaching upon the area of building lands. Such parkways, and also large parks, can often be made through wise planning and management to serve several of the purposes required of local parks for the adjacent territory, without interfering at all with the primary purpose for which they are intended. These connecting parkways will produce the effect of extending the parks over a much greater area and will provide approaches through which people may pass from their houses to the parks and from one reservation to another, without long tedious journeys through ordinary city conditions which tend very strongly to counteract or destroy the physical as well as the æsthetic benefits derived from a visit to the pleasure grounds.

The main arteries of the street system, if they are made broad enough to include trees and turf and other parklike features, do not differ essentially from parkways as above described, and it is to be hoped that, in those parts of the main thoroughfares which now lie in undeveloped regions favorable to such action, the city will secure sufficient width to give them a really parklike character. On the other hand, many of the routes indicated on the map and mentioned in the following section of this report as proposed parkways, may be expected ultimately to include electric car lines and other essentials of general traffic thoroughfares.

SPECIFIC RECOMMENDATIONS AND SUGGESTIONS.

In a general way the problems which should be considered, in the development and improvement of the city of New Haven, have been discussed in the preceding pages, where many recommendations are made both for immediate and for future action. The study of the city, upon which this general discussion with its recommendations is based, has involved also a detailed consideration of many of the specific problems, and has led to the preparation of the plan at the end of this volume, where, for convenience of reference, each problem is given a number, corresponding to the number in the following pages under which some statement is made of the special conditions which are involved. The reference to each problem is necessarily brief, however, and the list is far from complete, as in this report it would be impossible to lay down final, definite plans and details for the various problems of the city's development; but it is possible to outline a general scheme of improvement of which the details can be worked out as the needs shall require and as engineering necessities or economies dictate.

THE HEART OF THE CITY.

The Green, which has always been the center of the city, was surrounded in early days by the most important buildings; on three of the adjacent streets were placed the residences of the most important citizens and the various structures of civic importance, while the University gradually extended to enclose the fourth side. The beauty of the Green has survived through the various stages of civic development, and it was not until encroachments were suggested in recent years that the people awoke to the need of protective measures and of a careful study of the whole problem.

Locations must, of course, be found for important buildings both of civic and of private character. The frontage along the Green affording unobstructed light is naturally desired for such structures, and as the city has grown the need for more important buildings becomes obvious and imperative. New Haven now needs a new postoffice, a new commercial hotel, a new courthouse, a hall of records, and many other like buildings; it should have an adequate opera house, and a good market house. The need for a new library and a new courthouse are now being met. The postoffice, the hotel and other buildings would naturally group themselves about a civic center. Is the Green such a civic center? Can it be used as such without permanent loss to the city? Such buildings should be brought in fairly close relation to one another for convenience in the transaction of business. The postoffice, for example, should be located either at the station or in the heart of the business district; a combination of the two ideas would probably conduce to practical utility. Eventually the postal business of the city will be transacted more largely by substations, but nevertheless a postoffice located not far from the present position on Church Street will still be needed.

The congestion of streets must soon be relieved, either by the widening of individual streets or by providing a way for traffic to be deflected. Any effort to widen Church

No. 18.　Proposed civic center for Baltimore, including a railway station, a public market and other public buildings all facing on a parkway.

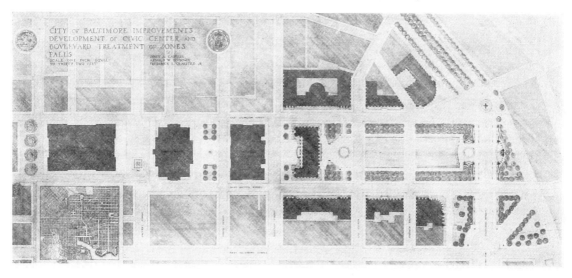

No. 19.　Plan for Baltimore civic center.

Street, where the densest traffic now exists, would involve immense expense and great disturbance of business interests, but, by increasing the width of Temple Street and thereby increasing its importance, a portion of the through travel which now goes by way of Church Street could be deflected to Temple Street, especially if the opening from Temple Street into Congress Avenue and George Street were made broader and more direct.

The junction of Congress Avenue with George, Church and Meadow streets is a natural center of interest. At or near this point must pass for many years a constant stream of traffic.　A new avenue from the new station to intersect Congress Avenue at a point where it would also be intersected by Temple Street if Temple Street were extended forms a logical center near the junction of Congress Avenue and Church Street.   The land is poorly developed, and this location in the heart of the city near to the station, near to the business, and not far from the residential section, is naturally one which might properly be considered for a secondary civic center.

The location of the new railroad station forms the third important feature in the problem at the heart of the city.   In accordance with the considerations in regard to traffic discussed under the head of "Main Thoroughfares and Car Lines," we have been led to prepare the accompanying plan (No. 32, page 59) and the following notes as to the relation of the three main features and the treatment of the problem as a whole.

The plan calls for a radical change, but the need for it can be realized when we consider that, so long as New Haven was a small town, with its business concentrated in the vicinity of the wharves and railway and its residential section in the neighborhood of the Green, the connection of its several parts by lines available for through traffic was comparatively unimportant; but with the city's growth, through lines of travel, unimpeded by the congestion of the more crowded central district, become more and more necessary, so that every part of the city can be readily and conveniently reached from every other part.

It is only by wise provision for the future as well as the present that the city's growth and development can be assured.   If the first cost alone is to be considered, or if the whole development is assumed at one time, the people of New Haven may well hesitate to enter into any extensive project of civic improvement; but if the first cost is balanced off against the increase in land values, the improved facilities for transacting business, the increase and betterment of population (well housed and well cared for), the added beauty and desirability of the city as a place of residence, and the civic pride of its people and consequent better citizenship, it will be worth the cost many times over.   If the project of civic improvement is undertaken along wise and conservative lines and carried forward on a well-defined programme, item by item, causing no general disturbance in values nor any appreciable increase in taxation, the cost need not be a burden upon the taxpayers and the benefit to the city will be immeasurable.

1. New Haven Green.

The New Haven Green has gone through a slow but steady process of evolution from a simple open field to a much traveled city square, with business crowded about it and paths crossing it in all directions.   If Temple Street is widened and the surrounding mall improved, it will probably require but few more changes in plan.   The plants and structures upon the surface, however, are destined to much more change as time goes on; the great trees are suffering badly from starvation, neglect and actual abuse; many of them will die in the near future and others may be restored only with great difficulty and at considerable expense; many new trees will be planted in the future and for these a definite plan of location and policy for planting should be made.   The simple system of regular rows, so long ago started and so appropriate, has been interrupted by new arrangements in planting.   The plan should be restored.

Across the lower end of the Green the new walks have been filled to be higher than the natural surface and a number of shapeless pockets are thus formed.   These should be regraded to fill them and they should be properly drained, as has been done already in part.

Another question which confronts the authorities and should be decided once for all, is that of structures, statues, and monuments on the Green.   The example of other cities and

No. 20.   View showing the vista which crosses the Green parallel to Temple Street.   If necessitated by the widening of Temple Street north and south of the Green, an additional road could be built here without destroying large trees.

the simple, dignified character of the Green itself, lead us to recommend that the policy be adopted of excluding forever from the surface of the Green all structures, except possibly a well-designed rostrum or music stand; and all gardens or so-called floral decorations should be prohibited.

The lights on the Green should be kept at a height of about 20 feet above the ground and the wires placed in underground conduits.   The lamp standards should be properly designed so as to give the best and most effective lighting and to be attractive features in themselves.

A public comfort station must be provided sooner or later, but this may well be placed below the surface, as in Boston and other cities.   It should, of course, be made as inconspicuous as possible.

The band stand should be rebuilt, of a simple dignified design more in keeping with the architecture of the fine old colonial churches, instead of remaining as at present an object which defaces the Green.

The churches should be restored to their original appearance. The texture and color of these colonial buildings is quite as much an essential of the design as the proportions and the architectural details. The paint should be removed from the brickwork and the woodwork painted white.

Consideration of the walk around the Green brings up a serious question of curb lines, trees and fences. The existing double lines of trees, forming as they do a bordering mall, should be completely restored and permanently maintained. This means that the curb must remain where it is; but the walk may well be moved into the center of the 45-foot space under the arch of trees, and enlarged to a 25-foot walk, with seats along the sides so placed as to serve as guards to prevent short-cutting where walks are not provided or intended.

No. 21. Walk at the Green.

The question of control over the character of the buildings surrounding the Green is a serious and perplexing one. It may as well be recognized at once that the growth of the city and the increase in land values of the property facing the Green, are creating economic conditions which lead to buildings of greater height and importance, and that private enterprise will inevitably change the whole aspect of the property within a few years. Unreasonable restrictions should not be attempted, but the common interest of all citizens requires that the city's historic center should not be defaced. Probably the only respect in which they can be directly and effectively controlled is by a limitation of height. Boston, with a much larger population, has found it possible to restrict the height of buildings facing Copley Square to 90 feet, and the wisdom thereof is apparent. Limitations of height are needed in all our cities, but they should be as flexible as is consistent with the thorough practical protec-

No. 22. View at the Green showing fence and walk crowded to one side of the space under the over-arching trees. A broad walk should occupy the center of this space.

tion of the common interest in light and air. In the case of the Green, any limitation of building height is not a question of light and air, but a purely æsthetic matter, and it appears to be one of those cases where a certain uniformity of height is greatly to be desired, in order to preserve an already established character. We advise, therefore, that a building height limitation not exceeding 100 feet be imposed by law upon the property fronting on the Green.

By limiting the height of buildings, the city will not only present a certain desirable unit at the skyline and add greatly to its beauty and dignity, but will also cause the development of business structures to spread more generally through the available business district; thereby enhancing the value of property over a wider area, and avoiding the congestion of traffic inevitable where high buildings are concentrated. Such limitation of height is, therefore, not an economic loss to a city, either in usage or in the total of property values, but is a direct economic gain to the city as a whole as well as to the larger number of its property owners. The height limitation might

No. 23. Architect's sketch for new Library facing the Green.

be made to apply to the property facing the Green, to the proposed new civic center, to the station plaza, and to the proposed new avenue leading from the station to the Green.

In Boston, buildings are limited in the business district to 125 feet in height above the sidewalk grade on the side of the principal entrance, in the rest of the city at large to 80 feet, and on the borders of most of the parks and parkways to 70 feet; with provision for roofs, steeples and other projections to rise above those heights upon approval of plans by the proper authorities. In Washington, and in most European cities, the height limitation is fixed in relation to street widths, as for example "20 feet higher than the width of the street"; or the streets are classified, e.g., 20 to 30 feet wide, 30 to 40 feet, 40 to 60 feet, etc., and for each class a standard height limitation is fixed. We are not prepared to say what is the best height limitation to adopt for New Haven at large, beyond saying that it should be flexible and differentiated,

No. 24. Design for the avenue that is now being built as planned to cut across St. Paul
to the new Capitol Building.

as, for example, according to the type and use of building, or amount of open space in connection with it, or part of city in which it occurs, rather than rigid and uniform for all buildings.

The treatment of Temple Street where it crosses the Green is considered below (p. 56).

2.   The Station Plaza.

With the erection of a great new station in New Haven the city should make some provision for proper approaches and surroundings.   At the entrance to the building, where pedestrians, street cars and carriages will congregate and where the incoming travel emerges, a

No. 25.   Architect's sketch for the Station which as now planned has no proper setting and no adequate line of approach.

generous open space is needed.   The first impression of most visitors to the city will be gained on emerging from the station; this impression may be followed by others, but the first impression is a lasting one and upon this impression will be largely based the opinion of the city as formed by its visitors.   An ample and agreeable vestibule to the city should be provided by New Haven and should be properly connected with the business section of the city beyond.

The buildings surrounding the station plaza should be limited in height to conform to the total height of the station.   These buildings should be adapted to the special uses incident to the neighborhood of a railway station, such as small stores or shops, cafes, station hotels, offices for express and transportation companies, postal station, etc., etc.   They might well be designed to have the ground story arcaded, so as to provide a sheltered passage from one shop to another.

3. Proposed Public Square.

The reasons for establishing a secondary civic center, at or near the intersection of Temple Street extended and Congress Avenue, have been given above. The form proposed is shown upon the plan, which provides admirable sites for public and semi-public buildings. Within the square provision should be made for a possible portal to a subway, which must in time be built and which could well enter here to take advantage of the favorable change in grade on Temple Street. Such a portal may be in a broad space and may be made not only unobjectionable but even attractive by proper architectural treatment, with arches and balustrades, and by proper provision for masses of planting.

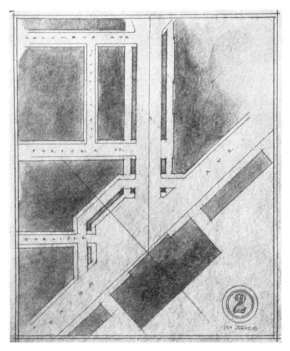

No. 26. Sketch for possible treatment for the Plaza in front of the Station.

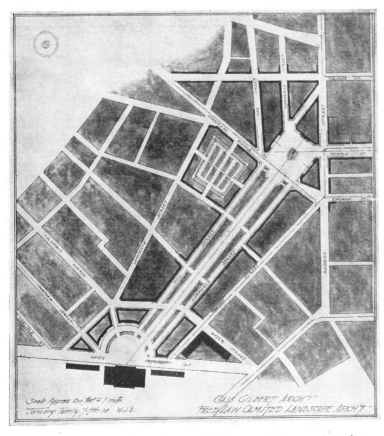

No. 27. Sketch for an Avenue between Hill Street and Commerce Street from the Station to the proposed Public Square. Later revised to move the Station westward. See Fig. 31.

4. Avenue from the Public Square to the Station.

The location of the new station west of the present one is made necessary by practical railway conditions, such as the curve of the track, the length of trains, and the governing grades. For practical reasons the tracks must be slightly higher at the platform to facilitate starting and stopping, and this cannot be made nearer the bridges which span the "Cut." To accommodate the branch roads long straight sidings must be made on the town side, so the station must be placed practically as already planned by the railroad company.

The narrow streets which lead to the present station will

be more indirect and more inconvenient for the new station, so that a new route will certainly be needed from the main distributing points of the city to the railway portal. The plan here recommended is intended to take advantage of present real estate conditions, to recognize all the growing conditions, and to produce a simple, dignified and economical solution of the many problems involved. Many other plans have been considered and others are possible, but we believe that in the long run the one proposed will prove the most economical, the most impressive, with its vistas at either end; and the most profitable with its opportunities for developing fine sites for commercial blocks on either side. (Fig. 31.) An avenue 120 feet wide through this part of the city, cutting through cheap lands, and opening up the property for development, although it will mean a considerable initial outlay, would justify itself upon a purely economic basis through the increase in land values along the route; but its primary justification is that it is a much needed practical and æsthetic improvement, the immediate cost of which is not beyond the city's means.

No. 28.   Sketch of treatment for proposed Public Square
(afterwards changed to include portal for subway).
See Fig. 31.

5.   Temple Street and the Subway,
and College Street Extension.

To connect the proposed square with the Green and the city beyond we have proposed that Temple Street should be widened, so as to carry a large amount of surface travel, and that beneath it should be constructed a subway to carry the north and south lines of local and suburban traffic through the heart of the city and across the east and west lines below grade. It is proposed to widen Temple Street on the southeasterly side only, because the buildings are less costly than those on the opposite side, and because any widening of Temple Street across the Green can best be done on the side away from the three churches. By widening on one side only, it is obvious that the expense may be kept at a minimum.

The cost of this improvement is likely to prove a large item, but is relatively small as compared, for instance, with the cost of widening Church Street between Chapel and George streets, and will, in our opinion, not only relieve in a large degree the congestion on Church Street, but will increase the value of Temple Street property materially.

We have indicated on the general plan the extension of College Street from the corner of Grove Street and Prospect Street to Whitney Avenue at its intersection with Temple Street, and also from its intersection at George Street through to Congress Avenue. We do not regard these extensions of College Street as a necessary feature of the plan. They would, however, provide an undoubtedly useful line of communication from the northerly section of the city to Congress Avenue and Washington Avenue and, by these routes to Allingtown and West

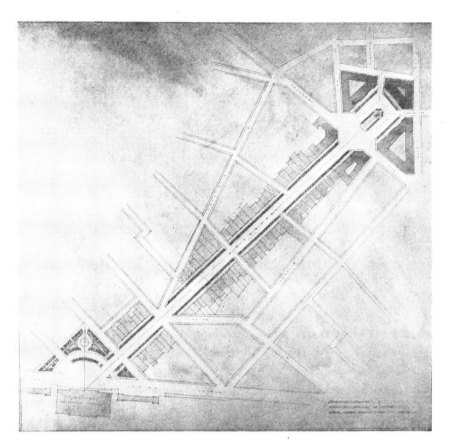

No. 29. Sketch for an Avenue 120 feet wide through a part of Water Street to the proposed
Public Square. Again changed somewhat in the plan as finally recommended. See Fig. 31.

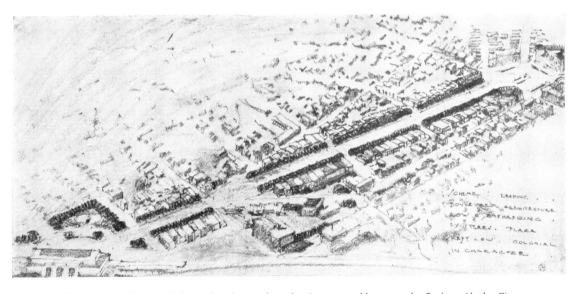

No. 30. Sketch view of above plan showing how the Avenue would connect the Station with the City.

Haven; and thus deflect some of the travel from Temple and Church streets. The southerly extension of College Street would unquestionably aid in the development of that section, now badly served by a complicated system of unrelated short streets. The extension of the northerly end of College Street is more doubtful, as it would require some special treatment in crossing Hillhouse Avenue and the Northampton "Cut" and would destroy expensive buildings of the Sheffield Scientific School.

THE GENERAL STREET SYSTEM.

The following suggestions for specific improvements in the thoroughfares of New Haven are to be regarded as supplementing the above general recommendations (page 20), to the effect that the existing main thoroughfares ought to be widened wherever such widening is still possible. The suggestions vary greatly in importance, but it has seemed more convenient to consider them in rotation according to their position on the map than according to relative importance.

6. Orange Street.

Orange Street provides a direct line from the Mill River district and East Rock Park to the center of the city. It offsets at Crown Street and extends thence one block to George Street. It might well be straightened from Crown to George Street by simply widening it in this block, and in time should be extended from George Street to intersect with Meadow Street. It would be better if such extension could be by a direct line passing through the Armory to the corner of Whiting and Meadow streets, but would practically serve the same purpose if deflected at the Armory so as to enter Meadow Street at a right angle.

7. Union Street Extension.

With the new station and with the increase in travel, the need for a proper connection between Union Street and Kimberly and Howard avenues will become greater and greater. To extend Union Street to the southwest will involve cutting through private property having some improvements upon it, but the importance of such a street for public purposes will become very great, and a considerable expense in securing it would be entirely justifiable.

The east end of Union Street should connect directly with the Water Street bridge over the railroad. As West Haven and East Haven develop, a large volume of traffic will be thrown upon the streets which make the circuit of the harbor by way of Tomlinson's bridge, Water Street, Union Avenue, and Kimberly Avenue, and the obstacles to free circulation on this route should be systematically removed now before they become any greater.

8. Kimberly Avenue Widening and Extension.

The main channel for travel from the city toward the southwest, for a long time at least, must be the street and viaduct of Kimberly Avenue. With the increasing growth now going on in and west of West Haven, and with the shore travel of autos to and from the western part of the state, New York and beyond, this avenue is already heavily taxed and relief must in time be provided. The possibility of a parallel street for relief is practically cut off by conditions of water fronts and railway routes, and the avenue itself must probably be widened. The policy of preventing the building up of existing front yards beyond the line of proposed future widening,

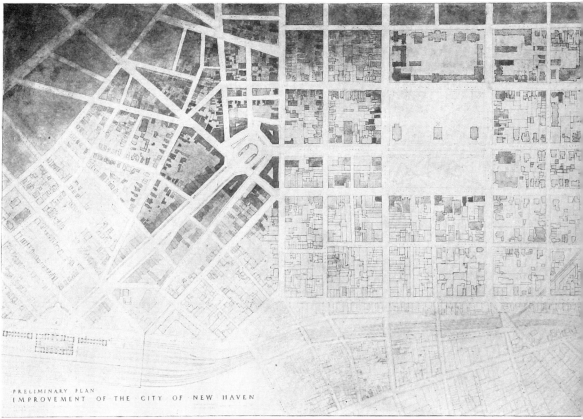

PRELIMINARY PLAN
IMPROVEMENT OF THE CITY OF NEW HAVEN

No. 31.

Birdseye view of proposed Avenue from the Station to the Green
through the proposed Public Square.

No. 32.

Plan as recommended for an Avenue from the Station to the Green, showing
also the proposed improvements in Temple Street and in College Street,
and the proposed site for a monument at Whitney Avenue.

as previously advocated, should be at once applied to this avenue, and to that end a plan for future widening should be at once adopted.

At West Haven, to facilitate travel, the avenue should be planned to extend through to the corner of Center and First streets. This extension, in connection with the extension of Center Street mentioned below, would give a route through West Haven free from car tracks, and it would give a much improved access by way of First Street toward Sandy Point.

The extension of Kimberly Avenue would damage the factory property at Elm Street, but it would be possible to allow the large brick building jutting out into the street location to remain until the demand becomes great enough to justify the cost of its removal.

This proposed extension may be affected somewhat by the shore development proposed and discussed under the paragraph on general shore conditions. (See pages 20 and 62.)

9. Center Street Extension.

To improve further routes to the southwest, Center Street in West Haven should be extended across the Cove River marshes. This extension may occur as an incident of the land subdivision, but may be blocked through shortsighted real estate openings unless it is definitely arranged for by public authorities. At the same time provision should be made for the direct continuation of Elm Street across the hollow which now interrupts its southwesterly course.

10. Edgewood Avenue Widening.

It has been proposed to raise and widen Edgewood Avenue across the river and widen it through Westville.* There appears to be no need of going to the expense of making the causeway 170 feet wide to correspond with the width of Edgewood Avenue east of the valley, because a single roadway of reasonable width, with side slopes pleasantly graded and planted as a part of the park, will answer every practical purpose and be equally agreeable. Attractiveness can here be secured by making the street in effect a part of the park, instead of by widening the street itself beyond the demands of traffic. In order to improve the grade at the west end the causeway should probably be somewhat raised; but every foot added to its height makes it more difficult to harmonize the embankment with the park landscape. The profile should be designed with a view to carrying a future park drive under the avenue at some point which will fit in with a complete general plan of park development.

Beyond the park the avenue is now narrowed down to the width of an ordinary street. This could well be widened to form a parkway, if the owners of adjacent lands are willing to meet a sufficiently large share of the cost, for which they would presumably be repaid through the increase in land values; but as a feature of the general highway system such a widening is of relatively small value. On account of the almost impassable hill beyond Forest Street at the west end and the lack of direct connections toward the heart of the city in the east end, Edgewood Avenue can never be expected to become a main thoroughfare and must be regarded as the highway of a relatively small district.

11. North Goffe Street Extension.

In connection with the development of Beaver Ponds Park and the adjacent streets, plans have been made for extending Sherman Avenue across Beaver Park Playground and along the

*Note: Since the above was written, Edgewood Avenue has been raised and a new bridge constructed.

east side of the park to Fruit Street.   We question whether the diagonal connection with Sherman Avenue is of sufficient importance to justify cutting the existing playground in two, but such a street along the east boundary of the park, continuing Fruit Street south to Munson and connecting through County Street with Goffe Street, is much to be desired.   Before the question is finally decided a further effort should be made to gain possession of the area between the park and the playground.

12.   Crescent Street and Fowler Avenue Improvements.

The improvement of Crescent Street has recently come under consideration.   A better connection toward the city can be made by widening north of Goffe Street and by widening Goffe Street on the playground side, and a better connection with both Wintergreen Street and Fowler Avenue toward the country can be made, as indicated on the general plan.   In reconstructing these streets along present and proposed park frontages, provision should be made for proper connection with pleasure drives through the park.

13.   Prospect Street Cut-off.

Prospect Street, leading out from College Street and the heart of the city, affords access to some of the most attractive private places.   It is a popular pleasure drive as far as it goes, but at the northern end it pitches steeply down and ends abruptly against Mill Rock.   This condition can be greatly relieved by cutting a diagonal street to the northwest to connect with the proposed parkways and to develop further attractive frontages in the area as yet unoccupied.

14.   Water Street Widening.

As one of the main teaming streets of the city, Water Street is destined to become more and more congested and to be the cause of much delay.   The present narrow street should be widened where possible sufficiently to give room for two wagons on each side of the car tracks, but the sidewalks may reasonably be left quite narrow.   East of the freight yards and docks, Water Street is choked by large factories and could be widened only at great expense.   There the travel is now comparatively small and until the bridge is improved and East Haven is more developed, the need for widening this part of the street will not become pressing.   Much of the frontage of Water Street, however, is either open or occupied by cheap wooden buildings, which are bound to give way to other structures, and this is emphatically a case where a widening should be planned and where action should be taken, as occasion demands it, to require the erection of all new buildings back of an established building line.

15.   Shore Treatment at Freight Yards.

The railway company holds a large tract of water front property opposite the heart of the city, well situated as a local freight yard, with track connections to two existing piers and more water front than is likely to be needed in connection with rail and water transhipments for an indefinite period into the future.   The development of the property for railroad purposes must cease when the company has filled to the bulkhead line.   It would seem highly desirable to provide for the ultimate construction of a broad street along the water front, connecting with Water Street at the northeast and with Howard and Kimberly avenues at the southwest.   Such a street would provide a convenient means of access to the freight yards, and would give to the public the use and control of a central portion of the water front, while, if properly designed, it need not interfere in any way with the business of the railroad.

16. Tomlinson's Bridge, Grade Crossing and Railway Rights.

The traffic in the southeastern quarter of the city is now seriously handicapped by the conditions obtaining at Tomlinson's bridge. Over this narrow bridge the railway company holds certain rights, the street cars have a route and all teaming and pleasure travel for a very large radius must pass; and yet the town end of the bridge has no proper approach and the entire travel is frequently blocked by freight trains at the grade crossing.

Plans have already been made for eliminating the grade crossing at a very considerable expense, which will relieve the congestion to some extent. But this improvement alone may serve only to make evident other serious obstacles, if the bridge approach is to be turned abruptly into the narrow streets where it terminates. Certainly proper connection should be made with Water Street, the widening of which is only a question of time.

If the district of East Haven is to be developed, provision must be made for free and rapid transportation, by all kinds of vehicles, to and from the heart of the city, the freight yards and the various factory districts. If the water front is to be made available for factories, provision should also be made for railway connections. The best route for such a railway is probably to be secured by properly widening this bridge and carrying a railroad track along its southerly side, where it may be kept entirely separate from the highway.

17. Blatchley Avenue Bridge.

In the future, when the water front of East Haven develops, there will be need for better connections and the probability of a bridge over the Quinnipiac River on the line of Blatchley Avenue should not be lost sight of. The street is wide and will form an important cross-town line.

18 and 19. Ferry Street Extension.

The present termination of Ferry Street in East Haven is inconvenient. Provision is needed for proper connection to the south and southeast, and this can best be made by cutting a new street, shown as No. 18, and by widening and extending the south end of what is now Quinnipiac Avenue past the west side of the reservoir and through land which is now open, but is being sold off in building lots and is destined soon to be occupied.

20. Quinnipiac Avenue Widening and Extension.

As the main street along the east side of the river, Quinnipiac Avenue should be made ample and convenient. North of Ferry Street it can be widened in connection with proposed shore improvements (see Sec. 65), and possibly turned across the slough near Ferry Street bridge. South of the bridge great commercial plants interfere with any immediate extension, but the need for an adequate street to the southwest, in connection with the further commercial development of the water front, is a serious one and ought to be considered. Whether it should be relatively near the water front or substantially on the line of the Manufacturers' Street Railway, can be determined only after careful studies and estimates. The best solution may even involve a viaduct over the existing water front properties.

21.   East Shore of the Inner Harbor.

We have been urged to recommend that the city acquire for a public reservation the entire eastern shore of the inner harbor from the bridge to Fort Hale Park.   After careful consideration we are led to recommend that most of this shore be left for commercial development and that the city make some effort to encourage such development.

While it may be possible for the city to acquire at relatively small expense the shore front and large tracts of marsh land, the cost of converting this into a park would be relatively great, as the land is low and the shore consists chiefly of mud flats, neither agreeable nor easily improved. But the great argument against making a park of this shore is, that it is well adapted to future commercial development and will be needed for that purpose, whereas other shore lands of less commercial value are available for park purposes and are much better for park development and use.   It would be a wise step, however, for the city to acquire this harbor frontage, and, when the time is ripe, to develop a broad commercial street with dock facilities; then to let the wharves under proper leases, reserving in a few places sufficient areas to provide for such local water front parks as would be used by the people of the neighborhood.   This sort of treatment would necessarily terminate at Fort Hale Park, where the inner harbor ends, and beyond which the shore conditions are entirely different.

22 and 23.   Forbes Avenue Straightening and Extension.

To still further facilitate development of the East Haven district, the main street from the city, Forbes Avenue, should be made as direct as possible.   To straighten it will mean that several of the houses along the present route must be moved, but as there is plenty of vacant flat land back of them, this can easily be done.   Beyond Granniss Corners, Forbes Avenue comes to an abrupt and dangerous termination in what is now a point of congestion.   Small houses are being rapidly erected in this vicinity and, before any more development takes place, the street should be extended to cross the marshes, so as to provide a direct main artery to relieve Main Street toward East Haven.

24 and 25.   Grand Avenue Revision and Extension.

Grand Avenue, crossing Fair Haven, is the most direct outlet from the city toward the east, but once across the Quinnipiac River it rises so steeply as to be practically useless as a main artery.   This difficulty can be overcome in either of two ways.   A deep cut can be made through the brow of the hill, which would provide the most direct route to the country beyond, but would involve a considerable expense in land damages and in cost of construction, or the route can be deflected to the north to cross the hill at a lower point, which would involve less cost for construction.   This might be planned for even to the extent of eventually relocating the bridge, when the time comes that it must be rebuilt.   Which may prove the better route is a question that can be determined only after careful plans and estimates have been made.   Farther out on the avenue proper connections are needed to the north and to the south to develop the outlying regions.

26.   Essex Notch Cut-off.

The road from the city toward Foxon through Essex Notch is now fairly good, but it must eventually be improved in line and grade at a number of points, and, to connect it more directly with the northern portion of the city, there should be a road across the marshes and farm lands from Middletown Avenue.

LOCAL PARKS AND PLAYGROUNDS.

27. *Wooster Square. (Area, 4.7 Acres.)*

Wooster Square, in the heart of the east side, is now a simple square filled with well-developed elms. It cannot be kept in turf, as grass must naturally be shaded out or trampled out by the many visitors. The greatest service this square can perform for the community will be as a playground. Like Jocelyn Square it should be provided with such apparatus as will draw from the neighborhood the children who are sorely in need of such provision. Like Jocelyn Square, it can have no great open spaces, as the great trees should be preserved and they cut the square into many small areas. These areas should be definitely divided and arranged for the use of the several classes of visitors, under a playground plan, in a manner similar to that recommended for Jocelyn Square in the following paragraph.

28. *Jocelyn Square. (Area, 3.1 Acres.)*

Jocelyn Square, a small open space cut into four triangles by diagonal paths and well shaded by regularly spaced trees, should be developed in large measure as a playground.

If the trees are to be preserved, as they certainly should be, no large open space will be available for big games and the kind of play permitted must be limited to those games which can be carried on in small spaces with safety to the players and to the other occupants of the grounds. To provide for the greatest good for the greatest number of people, it is necessary to consider first what space should be devoted to each of several classes of users: small children, boys, girls, the aged and infirm and the general public.

We have already been asked to prepare a plan for the first step in developing this playground. The plan was presented and the following recommendations were made:

The smallest children will be the most constant visitors. They will want but little space, but they need special apparatus—a wading pool, a few sand-boxes, an open area restricted against the invasion of older and rougher players, and some protection from wind and sun.

Older boys need heavier apparatus—swings, ropes, ladders, poles, slides, teeters, and various other provisions for exercise; and they would like also an open field where games, especially ball, can be played, but little provision for such games can be attempted on the square in question. As the playground is developed, more apparatus than is shown on the plan may be installed by extending the spaces toward the south along the sides of the square near the boundary fences.

A playground for girls should be provided for in much the same way as that for boys. Under proper supervision scups should be added to their outfit, but unless supervised these are quite sure to make trouble.

The grown-ups will join to a certain extent in the work of the boys and girls, but will want a generous space for rest, for promenading, for concerts and for other social gatherings. They should have some seats and walks from which to watch the work of active players. For them, however, little money need be spent until the needs of those less able to go to the more distant parks have been provided for.

No. 33. Jocelyn Square, where a bit of play apparatus has been well appreciated.

The aged and infirm must not be overlooked. Their wants are fairly simple, but are often forgotten. They should be protected from the active players in a space where they may sit quietly in the shade or in the sunshine. For them and for the grown-ups we have proposed that the entire center of the square be kept more parklike, neat and quiet and free from games.

For the general public, including all those above mentioned, certain provisions should be made. A band stand, a shelter with proper toilet facilities, and plenty of seats, will be needed. These can hardly be provided now, but must be included in plans for future development.

The apparatus called for on the plan is that which can be at once constructed. The sand boxes can be cheaply and easily made. The pool will be somewhat difficult to make cheap and satisfactory, as provision must be made to prevent leakage, either by the use of a puddled clay or a hard bottom. It must be so built as to do little damage to the trees, and this will probably mean that it must be chiefly above ground.

The slide, a most popular feature, can be so made as to provide space for a toolroom beneath.

Owing to the narrowness of the space available, only a single line of gymnastic apparatus can be used, but good frames of this character can easily be obtained from the Narragansett Machine Company. The giant stride, a simple but very popular affair, supported on a single pole, can also be obtained there.

No suggestion has been made for fencing in the grounds, as the cost of that would be prohibitive at this time, but the areas set aside for play should eventually be fenced in on all sides.

29. Trowbridge Square. (Area, 0.8 Acres.)

The small park on Cedar Street known as Trowbridge Square can to advantage be provided with some of the simplest playground apparatus.

30. West Haven Green. (Area, approximately 6.1 Acres.)

Like New Haven, each town nearby has grown up around a public green. The treatment to be given such an area, where the town still centers about it, is that recommended for the New Haven Green,—to keep it very simple and dignified, to exclude all gardenesque elaboration, to keep it free from all athletic apparatus, together with the bareness and shabbiness which are the inevitable accompaniment of a playground, and to prevent the introduction of buildings, monuments or other structures.

31. Scranton Street School Playground.

About the large school building on Scranton Street only a small area has been set aside for a playground. The surrounding block is now but little built upon and could well be acquired in its entirety as a much needed local playground.

32. Beaver Park Playground. (Area, 13.3 Acres.)

Reference has already been made (Sec. 11) to the possible cutting into the edges of Beaver Park Playground to improve the surrounding streets. This encroachment should be considered in connection with the plan for interior development. This playground, lying so near Beaver Ponds Park, may be devoted chiefly to outdoor gymnastic apparatus, baths and bare play space, except so much as may be needed to make the frontage on the important thoroughfares of Goffe and Crescent streets attractive.

33. Highwood Park.

There is now a small tract of interesting glacial formation in Highwood which is apparently used for park purposes. This should be reserved for public uses and eventually developed as a neighborhood park, with a portion of the area devoted to various kinds of play.

34. Chatham Street Playground.

To provide for a playground in the 12th Ward, the two blocks now practically vacant on Chatham Street could well be reserved. There are other possible sites nearby, but that shown is nearest to the fully occupied territory. The parkway and shore property already reserved and known as Clinton Park can be used for various recreative purposes, but in addition to these there should still be a large open space for play.

35. East Haven Green. (Approximate Area, 4.0 Acres.)

The future of East Haven Green will probably be much the same as that of West Haven above mentioned. The Green should be kept free from buildings, monuments and other structures.

36.   Fort Wooster Park.   (Area, 17.0 Acres.)

The small hill now set aside as Fort Wooster Park can be made somewhat more useful and attractive by removing some of the planting now at the foot of the slope so as to keep open the views from the ridge.

The summit of the hill·and the old fort command a fine view over the harbor, but if this is to be preserved a further tract should be acquired to the south and west.

37.   Quinnipiac Park.   (Area, 10.8 Acres.)

The small shore park in Fair Haven at the mouth of Mill River, if filled to the pier and bulkhead line, will contain a considerable area.   It can well be developed as a neighborhood playground.   In its development provision should be made for a bathing place, either a beach or a tank of considerable size.   The question of sewage contamination will have to be carefully considered in reference to the bathing facilities, pending such time as a comprehensive system of sewage disposal may be undertaken.

38.   Waterside Park.   (Area, 17.5 Acres.)

The shore park known as Waterside Park has already been filled and is now provided with some play apparatus.   No provision has yet been made for bathing, but this should be considered in the ultimate plan of the park.

39.   Bayview Park.   (Area, 23.4 Acres.)

One of the most attractive properties acquired by the city is that of Bayview Park at City Point.   This park, covering a relatively small area, is not large enough to become a general seashore recreation ground, but it is in a good position to provide an outing place for a considerable section of the city.

40.   Kimberly Avenue Playground.

Near Kimberly Avenue School a tract of a few acres of marsh land and other unoccupied property could well be acquired now before buildings are erected which would be costly to remove.   This land would serve the local needs of the community now growing up around it and would make a good playground for the schools nearby.   This is fairly near Bayview Park, but it would be practically all playground, and the former may well be kept as a more quiet and more decorative park.

INNER CIRCUIT OF PARKS, PARKWAYS AND RESERVATIONS.

41-45.   The West River and Edgewood Park.

Between Whalley Avenue and the harbor the winding channel of West River makes its way through a long belt of marshy ground, salt marshes in the lower course of the stream and fresh or brackish marshes in the upper reaches.   The tides have been excluded by a dike and gates at the Congress Avenue bridge, which serve to prevent submersion of the land and to permit a system of drainage sufficient to render the marshes usable for hay lands.

The heavy floods which formerly came down the West River in spring freshets are now greatly diminished by the storage reservoir of the waterworks, and under proper management there is no reason why the West River marshes can not be made into excellent park meadows, broad, smooth, fertile and dry enough at most seasons to be freely used for every park purpose. On the other hand, if these lands are to be used for building land it will be necessary, on account of sewerage conditions, to put in an enormous amount of filling. The cost of such filling, if attempted at once, would be prohibitive, while the slow process of filling as a dump will mean many years of hideous dumps and unproductive property, with, in all probability, a poor class of occupancy in the end. For these reasons and because the adjacent parts of the city are not provided with local park spaces, we advise the acquisition of practically all the marsh land along the river north of the Berkshire Division Railroad. South of that the marshes between the railways will have relatively small park value and will probably be needed for commercial or for railroad

No. 34. Marshes of the West River that should be preserved as park scenery.

purposes, and south of the main line railroad the marsh will certainly be needed for commercial purposes.

In connection with acquiring the marsh we advise so far as possible the acquisition of the banks that enclose them, for wherever possible the bluffs overlooking the marsh should be kept in park, and space enough should be acquired above the bank for a boundary road.

One very serious problem that confronts the city, regardless of the future of the marshes and of the river, is that of the proper disposal of the sewage now allowed to wash into the stream through the storm overflows of the city sewers. This problem, already discussed in the paragraph on the sewerage problem, is becoming more and more serious every year, and must in time be met by the city.

The present area of Edgewood Park has already been somewhat developed for park uses, but there still remains much to be done to bring it to a state of completion. As now planned it is to be devoted to general park purposes, with provisions for playfields, driving and boating; but the plan can be much improved upon to bring out the real charm of the valley landscape, to improve the somewhat awkward and uninteresting lines of the slopes and shores, and to produce more pleasing outlines and masses of foliage. The park may in fact be made to have much the same character as that of the Riverway in Boston, as illustrated under the discussion of Beaver Ponds Park, and to have the added charm of large open areas to be used as playgrounds or meadows. The causeway of Edgewood Avenue is one of the most conspicuous blemishes of the existing scenery, and its inharmonious character should be modified by properly planned grading and planting of its slopes. Much of the needed improvement can be gradually accomplished in connection with the annual maintenance, if a definite and comprehensive plan is adopted and followed.

46. West River Mills.

In the valley of the river between Whalley Avenue and West Rock Park, a considerable area should be acquired to preserve as far as possible the landscape value of this portion of the stream, and to provide for a broad street and parkway through Westville up the river to the proposed parkways (Secs. 82, 83). It should be possible to acquire most of the land through negotiation with the owners of factories and mill privileges, and still to avoid any serious interference with the industrial and commercial uses of the land in the neighborhood.

This matter should not be long delayed, as it may be seriously blocked by the growing development of small houses in the neighborhood.

47. West Rock Park. (Area, 215.3 Acres.)

The large tract known as West Rock Park is chiefly a great reservation of wild rugged slopes and cliffs. The great cliff, rising in a sheer precipice nearly 300 feet high, makes a very impressive sight as seen from the end toward the city. The fringe of trees at top and bottom and the dotted specimens upon the face of the cliff add much to the rugged charm of the spot. At the base of the cliff there has formed naturally a large mass of talus from the crumbling cliff. This talus has in places been removed to a very considerable degree, with a consequent apparent increase in the height of the cliff. At one point stone crushers have been for a long time at work, but these are soon to be removed. Before blasting is stopped, however, some consideration should be given the ultimate plan; for, at the point where quarrying has been done, and the natural condition scarred and altered, it would be desirable, in order to bring out the greatest effectiveness of the cliff, to remove thousands of tons more of the low lying rock.

Some efforts have been made to render the area accessible and in places to make it parklike. The work so far has been in general well planned, but in some details it is very unfortunate.

No. 35. West Rock Park Drive near Judges Seat, showing steps where a grade walk would be less conspicuous and less dangerous than steps.

The drive is retained in places by smooth laboriously paved banks, that are quite out of keeping with the surroundings and that prevent the natural growth on the slopes and compel the maintenance of costly and undesirable fences. This paving should be torn up and the slope filled over with soil and planted to trees and shrubs, with a few large rocks here and there. There is no reason why natural conditions should not be restored to the very wheelways, and no definite line need be maintained to mark the edges of the road. Where the fence must remain as a matter of safety, it should be provided with a hub board, as otherwise it will serve to wreck the vehicles it is intended to protect.

Near the top there is a long detour to the west that is forced and unnecessary, serving only to reach a view that is far inferior to the view from the summit. The road had better come upon views naturally and follow routes that appear reasonable.

The character of maintenance at the summit appears out of keeping with the grand ruggedness of the hill. The brush should not be mown down, but only such bushes as actually block the view should be cut; more trees should be cut now, to develop actual views, and others should be replanted, or allowed to grow up where trees have been removed from points that need not be kept open. The rare and interesting native plants should be protected, and smooth turf and exotic looking plants such as the Yucca should be entirely excluded. The summit of the rock should be kept free for all time from structures; no shelter or building should be allowed to appear in the view of the rock from the city.

Along the base of the great cliff no path should be allowed, as rock frequently falls there. The talus slope should be left rough and unbroken and travel should be confined to a path near the brook at the base.

The paths up the hill, and those on the summit where in places they are supported by carefully laid walls at either side, are ugly and actually dangerous; the walls should in many places be removed, or else the land at the sides should be filled upon to the level of the walks.

The western boundary of the park is unfortunately placed in relation to the slope of the land and to the possible views. The lines should be relocated before the settlement now begun has spread any farther.

A proposition has been made to carry a trolley line to the summit of West Rock. This would be very unfortunate, as the summit is hardly suited to uses by great crowds, and the greatest value of the rock as a place of public resort lies in its rugged scenery and in the sense of wildness and remoteness to be obtained so near the city—a quality which would be largely destroyed both by the presence of a trolley line and by the concentration of crowds and the inevitable provisions for the comfort and amusement which would follow. The plea has been made that only the rich can get to the top. This is true only of driving to the top; and the fact is that the keenest enjoyment of the peculiar scenery of West Rock is to be felt only by those who make the steep climb on foot. The pleasure of mountain climbing does not consist solely or chiefly in being at the summit for a few minutes, but in the climbing itself and in the state of mind and body which is produced by climbing to the top amidst rugged and wild surroundings. This kind of pleasure is as open to the poor as to the rich, and it is the special kind of pleasure which West Rock can afford forever to the people of New Haven, if it is not spoiled.

The crowds which might gather on the summit if a trolley line were built thereto would assuredly get pleasure from the excursion and their number would doubtless be greater than that of the climbers, but the gregarious kind of pleasure which most of them would get could be obtained substantially as well at a beach resort, or at any good electric railway park on a

No. 36.   West Rock Drive, showing crude and dangerous drain inlets.

pleasant hillside, whereas the presence of the railway and the crowds would destroy much of the irreplaceable and peculiar value which the rock can give to those alone who appreciate it.

The drive to the summit might well have a few adjustments. The long uphill pull on a uniform grade should be broken with a few rests. Elsewhere it could be made steeper in places to avoid the tortuous circuits, except where fine views are to be developed. The provision for drainage is rather crude and conspicuous; the inlets could well be masked by the use of a few large boulders and some simple planting of native growth. There is an unfortunate lack of big picturesque boulders along the way, as apparently all the natural ruggedness has been effaced in getting material for road building. This cannot well be restored, but the practice should be rigorously guarded against in future construction. The sole purpose of the road being to exhibit scenery, the scenery ought not to be needlessly injured or reduced in the process.

48.   Springside Valley.

Above Westville the narrow valley along Springside Avenue should be acquired in order to connect the proposed Pine Rock Reservation. The land is now very attractive and is suitable for use as a park for many years to come without costly improvements. The cost of the land should not be very great, as it will require considerable grading and costly brook improvements to make it suitable for building purposes.

No. 37.   Springside Valley and vicinity, as yet little marred by urban encroachment.

No. 38.   What development under private control has done for a similar valley in another city.   A waste of natural resources.

No. 39. Springside Avenue from the northeast, showing private land, intervening between this point of view and West Rock Reservation, which it is proposed to acquire before additional buildings are erected.

49. *Beaver Brook Parkway.*

To connect Beaver Ponds Park with the West River Parkway and West Rock Park, a parkway should be extended up Beaver Brook. It should be wide enough to provide for a drive on each side and to include the tree-covered slope on the north side of Beaver Ponds Lane. In order to make this route short and direct, it has been suggested that, between Farnham Street and Fitch Street, just south of Beaver Ponds Lane, the parkway should be extended to the Springside Valley and that Beaver Brook be turned through this to shorten very considerably its length. This will permit of filling the old valley and improving the streets in that region.

50. *Beaver Ponds Park. (Area, 93.3 Acres.)*

There seems to be in New Haven an impression that Beaver Ponds Park is a wretched, dirty, hopeless boghole. Dirty it is and boggy; but far from hopeless, if it is to be improved in a thorough and systematic way. The present conformation of the ground presents many graceful and pleasing areas which can be preserved just as they are. Before the park can be made useful two essentials must be provided: the sewer outfall, which is destined soon to flood the valley with diluted sewage in times of storm, must be diverted down stream, and the swampy ground must be drained by tiles, or an open ditch deep enough to afford underdrainage through the park and into Beaver Brook beyond.

The plans for boundary streets for this park are already under consideration. The plan on the east contemplates a fill in several places, which will reduce the pleasant irregular slopes to a steep embankment that will be rather unsightly and difficult to treat. This street should be pushed back, if possible, especially near Munson Street. Beyond Fruit Street the street may be kept back as planned, but a second drive should be carried out near the top of the bluff.

No. 40. Riverway at Longwood in 1892, showing the uninteresting character of the grounds when graded but not flooded and not yet planted.

No. 41. Riverway at Longwood as now covered with trees and shrubs, fifteen years after construction.

No. 42. Riverway near Brookline Village, showing narrow reservation and unattractive character of surroundings.

No. 43. Riverway near Brookline fifteen years later, showing complete screening of surroundings and charming park-like character of the valley.

At the northwest the park should be extended far enough to include the steep banks and to provide for a border drive on the upland.

The accompanying illustrations of what has been done in the relatively narrow valley of the Muddy River on the line between Boston and Brookline are suggestive at least of what can be made of the area of Beaver Ponds Park.

No. 44.   Pine Rock Cliffs still undefiled and the foreground not yet blocked by such buildings as those now encroaching upon the foot of East Rock.

51. *Pine Rock.*

Pine Rock, as one of the four great ledges back of New Haven, should be preserved forever as a public reservation. Its value for recreation at present will be comparatively small, but as the city grows this value will increase. The value of the rock for other purposes is just now greater than for public recreation, but that value will probably not increase proportionately.

To remove the entire ledge would afford a large quantity of stone to the city and would eventually make good building sites. It is almost inconceivable, however, that more than a small part of the rock can be blasted away before the growth of the city leads to the erection of houses upon the adjacent lands. Whenever buildings begin to crowd in upon the skirts of the rock, the danger to life and property from the blasting will become so great as to require precautions and to impose methods of work that will render the quarries unprofitable. This will leave the remaining property partly as waste land fitted for no economic use whatever, and partly a site for a poor class of buildings on steep, inconvenient streets, relatively costly to build and to maintain—a district of low value both to its owners and to the city at large.

To acquire the rock for a reservation does not mean that quarrying need be stopped at once. In fact, it is possible that, in accordance with some definite plan, the quarrying might continue many years in such a way as to leave the property at the end of the operation in a condition to be even more available for the purposes of a public park than it is now.

If the rock is to be taken for a public reservation, the boundaries for taking are in part predetermined. The adjacent streets on the east and west, Wintergreen and Fowler, will become important radial streets from the heart of the city to the lands beyond and as such must

No. 45.   Pine Rock from the same point, showing devastation that cannot proceed far before the approaching city will make blasting impossible.

sooner or later be amply widened and possibly straightened.   Between each of those streets and the base of the rock space enough for a pleasure-way—whether for carriages or for pedestrians only—should be reserved.   This space should be not less than 60 or 80 feet in width between the foot of the rock and the highway in the narrowest places.

South of the rock a considerable space of level ground should be taken and kept open, to form a proper setting for the cliffs and to provide an ample playfield.   At the outer edge of this space should run a pleasure-way from which to obtain the best views of the rock, and outside of the pleasure-way a street for building frontage.

On the north slope of the rock the reservation should extend far enough to provide for a pleasure-way and for a boundary street that would accommodate cross traffic on easy grades. This would enclose a portion of the sloping fields, where some forms of active recreation can eventually be provided for.

This reservation should eventually be made to connect properly with the proposed extensions of Edgewood Park and West Rock Park in Springside Valley and with the proposed parkway eastward by way of Mill Rock to East Rock.   In addition to its intrinsic park value, therefore, Pine Rock has great importance as one of the links in a general park system.   The outline on the general plan indicates approximately the area that should be acquired, subject to some modification (a) depending upon the location of property lines and the result of negotiations with owners, and (b) controlled by the details of the topography as bearing upon the most economical and satisfactory lines of construction for realizing the general purposes set forth above.

52. Highwood Parkway.

East from Pine Rock there should be provision for a parkway of considerable importance into Highwood to form a link in the proposed inner circuit. The exact location of such a parkway through a fairly level country must depend largely upon real estate prices and conditions, but the proposed line should be fairly direct from Pine Rock Reservation or from Beaver Ponds Park to Mill Rock. One important question on this line must not be overlooked, and that is the question of crossing the railway tracks near Dixwell Avenue, and one advantage of the line as proposed is that the existing subway at the point where it is proposed to cross the tracks can be made use of. The line of parkway, as proposed, should not prove costly if acquired now, as it crosses an area that is practically vacant. This area is already cut into building lots, however, and destined soon to be reached by the building operations nearby and any delay in acquiring the route will certainly mean an increase in cost.

East of the railway tracks this route joins the forest reservation of the Winchester Repeating Arms Company, a reservation which is exceedingly attractive as seen from the street and which will probably so remain under the management of the company. If that reservation is ever acquired by the city, the proposed parkway will relate very properly with it.

53. Winchester Lakes Reservation.

The large tract of land which includes a portion of Lake Whitney, now fenced in by the Winchester Repeating Arms Company and used for the storage of explosives, and which we have for convenience of reference called Winchester Lakes, lies near the city and upon a line of fairly active growth. It will probably in time become too valuable for its present usage, and in that case a considerable portion, if not the entire area, could well be set aside for a public park. The enclosed body of water constitutes practically the only fresh water lake of any considerable size within many miles of New Haven that can be disconnected from the water supply system and used for public recreation. It can be cut off from Lake Whitney by a dam and can be drained around Mill Rock to a point below Lake Whitney. This would provide a large body of water for boating and skating which could be made easily accessible from all parts of the city. The charming little hills and hollows surrounding the lakes are well covered with timber, and so long as the land is used as at present this timber is likely to be preserved and protected.

Charming as the Winchester property is and large as its park value would be, it can probably not be made available for public use for a long time to come owing to its peculiar value for its present uses. In time, however, its value for park purposes, like its value for building purposes, will grow until it finally exceeds its industrial value to the company; and it is to be hoped and planned for that when the time arrives the city will acquire it rather than permit it to go upon the market for subdivision.

54. Winchester Parkway.

From the proposed Highwood Parkway along the south side of Winchester Lakes Reservation a parkway is needed to Mill Rock and eventually to East Rock Park. The parkway as proposed through the existing little valley and up to the end of Mill Rock will cross several lots having small houses upon them and will involve some filling, but most of the way it passes through land now undeveloped and in need of proper street openings.

55. Mill Rock and Possible Eastern Parkway.

Mill Rock, like Pine Rock, can never be wholly removed by quarrying, for it is even now practically surrounded by houses which would be damaged by blasting. It has little value for ordinary building sites, but as a public reservation it would preserve a generous open space and form an important link in the proposed park system. The water company holds a small area at the summit which need not be interfered with; the one house on the top could well be preserved to be used for park offices. The boundaries should be determined in detail to provide as far as possible for boundary streets on good grades.

The southern boundary should include the bench of fairly level land, upon which a drive can be carried eastward to meet Whitney Avenue north of the dam, and from which eventually a bridge can be constructed over Whitney Avenue and over the dam to the drives in East Rock Park. Such a bridge would form a direct connection between the two parks at the narrowest point and would provide a route free from interference of the congested travel on the avenue. The cost of such a bridge would be at this time prohibitive, but the ultimate need for it should not be disregarded in the city plans.

56-61. East Rock Park and Mill River Marshes. (Area of Park, 381.7 Acres.)

It is needless for us to descant upon the charms and beauties of the great cliffs and ridges of East Rock and upon the great advantage that will come to the city through the preservation of this splendid bit of wild and picturesque scenery, at the very door of the city, under such public control that it may continue forever to afford endless enjoyment and refreshment to the people.

In dealing with the problems of development and maintenance of the park, much work has already been done and thereby this great park has been rendered useful and accessible to the people. This development, however, is not yet completed, and in connection therewith three distinct problems have arisen that call for special and serious consideration. One of these concerns the general policy that should be established to control all further work of development and of maintenance, one relates to the improvement of boundaries of the park, and the third involves the much mooted question of the proposed lake in the marshes.

Three principal methods of treatment for the marshes and the Mill River Valley have been considered. To maintain the river as it now is, as a tidal estuary through which the harbor water flows in and out with every tide, involves serious objections which will increase as the water becomes more and more polluted from the city waste and as it carries into the river and the park more and more debris. The marshes, while not seriously injured in looks, will be kept in their present soft condition by the occasional high tides that flood them and thus their use for pleasure purposes will be prevented. The continual rise and fall of tide will expose at every fall the slimy mud banks and accumulating filth. With the further increase in adjacent city occupancy these conditions will tend to become intolerable, and sooner or later will force a series of costly changes similar to those which have followed invariably in other cities where like conditions have been allowed to continue for a sufficient length of time; namely, the eventual replacement of the banks by vertical walls and the filling of the adjacent lands at heavy expense, followed on private land by the erection of buildings. Buildings on all the private marsh land now vacant near the base of East Rock would be a great injury to the scenery, and the walling of the channel and filling of the marshes in the portion kept as park would be inharmonious as well as very costly.

To prevent such a future for the valley of Mill River it is possible to control the water by a dam at State Street or at Willow Street.

A dam across the lower end of the valley just high enough to prevent the water from falling much below the level of mean high tide would be the cheapest form to construct, would reduce the amount of fluctuation and keep the objectionable flats and mud banks covered, and would thus obviate the necessity of embankment walls. It would still leave much to be desired, however, as it would not keep out the high tides which submerge the flats and render them practically useless. It would, therefore, still be necessary to dredge the shallow flats, in order to maintain deep water where submerged, and to fill the low marshes to a point above the level of high tides. This plan would be open also to serious sanitary objections, because of the frequent and violent changes in the character of the water. Every run of spring tides would pour into the basin over the top of the dam large quantities of salt water to mix with the fresh or brackish water of the basin. Every freshet of the stream, especially if it occurred during a run of neap tides, would greatly reduce the salinity of the water. Such fluctuations in the character of the water would produce a serious nuisance through killing off the forms of plant and animal life upon which the self-cleansing power of the water depends. Thus, instead of affording a pleasant lake above the dam, this treatment would probably give rise to serious pollution through the gradual accumulation of a foul sludge of putrescent organic matter.

No. 46. Mill River from State Street Bridge. This view may be preserved and the marsh reclaimed as park land by placing the proposed dam at State Street.

A far better solution, but one involving a greater initial outlay, would be that based upon the principles recommended in the report submitted to the Board of Aldermen on October 1, 1902, by a committee of which Mr. Edward I. Atwater was chairman. Although we cannot support all the conclusions of that committee, we believe the principle to be a sound one and we recommend its adoption. A dam should be built across the lower end of the estuary in such a way as to shut out altogether the tidal waters, and to form a fresh water basin. If the normal level of this basin is fixed slightly below the level of the present salt marshes, the marshes may then be drained and converted into meadows without the cost of filling, and the banks of the stream under such a treatment can be made clean and agreeable at a relatively slight expense. Whether the river should be widened by dredging to form a lake, or kept as a winding river, is relatively a small matter and one that may be determined later, for the river can be used first just as it is, and can be developed later under a definite park plan.

The success of this treatment will depend upon the inflow of sufficient fresh water to offset evaporation in the summer time. This question was fully discussed in the report of Mr. Atwater's committee mentioned above, and convincing reasons were given for assuming that an adequate supply of water would be forthcoming through leakage and occasional flow over the Whitney dam, through use in the turbines and through minor tributaries and the various springs in the valley itself. In addition to the sources mentioned by this committee, there is perhaps another to be considered. The city, as riparian owner on the stream below the dam, should be able to require the water company to permit enough of the natural flow to pass the Whitney dam to prevent damage to its property.

Another difficulty to be met in the execution of this plan, not adequately considered by Mr. Atwater's committee, is that of dealing with the large volume of fresh water which will at certain times be poured into this relatively small basin, while the tide in the harbor is above the level of the water behind the dam. When the reservoirs on the stream above have been filled to their utmost capacity and the full volume of a spring freshet pours over the Whitney dam at the same time that high tide closes the tide gates below, the water in the proposed basin will rise rapidly and will not improbably flood the meadows. This occasional flooding may be provided for and the plans of park development be so adjusted that the damage will be slight; but the tide gates must at any cost be made large enough to allow the water thus impounded to run off at ebb tide. The design of tide gates in such a manner as to ensure a sufficient carrying capacity for the maximum floods, to ensure against their being obstructed by ice, and to render them easily and properly regulated, can be fixed only after careful study by an hydraulic engineer; but the estimates for this work submitted by the committee above mentioned would seem to be far too low to cover the cost of a structure that will meet the maximum requirements of the situation and that will protect the city against the risk of serious disaster.

An area of about 150 acres in extent, with its surface about one foot below mean high tide, will be shut up over four hours during a high tide. If the flow of 8,000 cubic feet a second, estimated as a possible maximum by the water company, should come over the dam, it would soon flood the area to above high tide level, and then overflow through the gates. As the tide goes down, eight or ten million cubic feet of water, in addition to the continuing flow of the stream, must be let out; and this will require tide gates to carry during the next eight hours an average of slightly over 8,000 cubic feet per second. In the valley of the Mystic River at Medford, Massachusetts, the new tide gates at Craddock's bridge are capable of letting through 6,000 cubic feet per second. This valley has a watershed slightly greater than that of the Mill River, but behind the dam, instead of a marsh area of only 150 acres on which to store the floods, as at Mill River, there are 350 acres of water surface and vast areas of relatively low lands besides, over which a slight flood will do but little damage. It would seem probable, therefore, that in New Haven the tide gates must be larger than those in Medford. The tide gates and sluices in Medford were built of reinforced concrete, without any architectural adornment whatever, at a cost of about $75,000.00, and this included only such excavation as was required at the gates themselves. In contrast to this, Mr. Atwater's committee proposed to build the gates and dam, and to do a very large amount of grading, for sixty or seventy thousand dollars. While we believe the estimates of the committee were too low, we are satisfied that this general plan offers the best and on the whole the most economical solution of the problem, and we advise that steps be taken to have detailed plans and estimates prepared by an hydraulic engineer and a landscape architect working in coöperation.

Before the site of the dam is definitely fixed at Willow Street, we would urge upon the city the desirability of placing the dam at State Street, as commerce will probably never come beyond that street and as the stream above that point is becoming a nuisance.

If sufficient funds are not forthcoming to do the whole thing thoroughly well at once, it would be far better to postpone the grading and to spend all the funds now available in obtaining the necessary and desirable lands, and in building ample permanent tide gates. With the permanent water level a foot or so below the marsh level, there would be no serious objection to delaying the costly work of grading.

Before any excavation or filling is done, the precise outline of the future water surface and the precise disposition of the excavated material should be studied in detail by a landscape architect, in order that the result may have the full landscape value attainable for a given expenditure. It would be very easy, indeed, to do the work in such a way as to be out of harmony with the striking and peculiar landscape of the rock and its lower slopes. Indeed, it would be very difficult to make any such new and wholly artificial feature to harmonize with the great rock as beautifully as do the natural salt marshes and the winding tidal creek. It is only because of the impracticability of permanently preserving the natural beauty of these marshes and this winding creek in the midst of a growing city, that we advise any changes at all. To the artist's eye the soft levels of salt marsh with their little pools of water, the winding creek with its exquisite natural curves, the shadows along its banks, the gleam of light here and there from wet banks of mud, together make a more beautiful middle distance over which to see East Rock than any new park lake is likely to offer. But slime and stagnant mosquito pools and moist salt marshes, however beautiful in the middle distance of a picture, are impossible as permanent features of a public recreation ground in the midst of a large city. In meeting these practical problems it must not be forgotten for a moment that it is a great picture, or series of pictures, that is here being retouched and modified—pictures for which thousands of dollars have been paid and the real value of which depends upon the degree of artistic imagination and skill with which the practical mechanical operations of alteration and maintenance are guided.

This brings us to the matter of the policy which should govern the management of East Rock Park. The policy that has controlled the management of the tract in the past, judging from the results, has been most admirable. The unsophisticated wildness of the area has in general been most judiciously preserved and simply made accessible by roads and paths. For the most part these ways appear to have come pretty close to the ideal requirements for ways in such a region, namely, that they be so placed as to lead people without undue effort and without danger or discomfort to the most agreeable points of view, that they be substantially built so as to minimize the cost of maintenance, and that from the very edge of the traveled way the surface of the ground and the vegetation which it bears should appear to be of a single piece with the rest of the work of Nature. There may be many frank evidences of human work, but so far as possible they should be of such character and so treated that Nature can adopt them as her own and harmonize them with the ground and rocks and natural vegetation. There are places where this principle has not been successfully followed, and experience elsewhere points to the danger of a gradual impairment of the essential landscape quality of the tract if these isolated instances are allowed to remain and to be repeated. The gardenesque quality in the treatment of certain spots, where planting of alien aspect has been used, strikes a discordant note against which Mr. Mitchell sounded a warning in his report of 1882. Because it is conspicuous, the false note struck by the shelter at the summit of the cliff is particularly unfortunate. Seen from below, projected against the sky, its slight and flimsy look is altogether out of keeping with the great crag on which it stands, and its very presence there diminishes the apparent height and impressiveness of the cliff, which would be magnified by the stunted growth of vegetation at its summit were it not for the contradictory scale of the shelter.

To enumerate other instances would be wearisome, for each one in itself would seem of trivial importance; but it is the summation of innumerable little details that are just right or that

No. 47. East Rock seen across the proposed ball-field. If not acquired by the city, this field will soon be covered with the cheap "double deckers," now actually encroaching upon the foot of the rock nearby.

just fail to be right, which makes the difference between scenery that is a subtle source of inspiration and refreshment, and a "park" that is only a place to go to take the air.

Only one other point needs mention in connection with East Rock—the matter of extension. We cannot too strongly urge the completion of the area to the north, out to the Ridge Road and to Davis Street, as urged by Mr. Mitchell in 1882. This would add to that end of the park a much needed piece of ground fit for athletic games and the gathering of large numbers of people; for with all its value as a preserve of picturesque scenery, the main body of East Rock Park does not provide space for the playing of games, and, foot for foot, will accommodate a far smaller number of people than if it were a tamer kind of park on fairly level ground; and the city will in time sorely feel the need of supplementing it.

Again, at the south end it seems to us of the utmost importance to acquire the bench or terrace of nearly level ground at the base of Indian Head. It is largely used to-day as a play-

No. 48. The "double deckers" now actually cutting into the very base of the rock and spreading to cover all available land.

ground, although the population within easy reach of it is only a small fraction of what it will be in another generation. New buildings are crowding up to the very edge of it and in a short time, if it is not acquired by the city, it will be covered with flat-houses, all contributing their quota of children and young men, who will need play and exercise but will have no place to get it, except such as the city provides.

Partly with a view to securing control of the cheap salt marsh lands which can in the course of time be converted into additional much-needed meadows, and partly in order to preserve a beautiful view of East Rock from the chief thoroughfare of the northeastern quarter of the city, we advise the acquisition of the salt marshes down to State Street, at which point we believe the proposed dam ought to be placed.

In the development of the proposed valley addition to the park area, provision could be made if desired for a speedway for horses. A more favorable situation for such a speedway, however, can be found in the broader valley of the West River, which we recommend should be acquired. In that location it would not be open to the objection of impairing the landscape effect of so important a view as that of East Rock.

62. Parkway over Railroad.

The great reservation of East Rock has been so developed that one of its main entrances is at the southeast corner, very near the broad valley of the Quinnipiac; but it is shut off from that and the country beyond by the new railway "Cut" and by the busy traffic of State Street. To connect this entrance properly, a costly viaduct would be necessary over the railway and possibly over the street also. Such an undertaking cannot reasonably be attempted by the city at present, but provision for this connection should be made and such lands as are needed should be acquired now in advance of building and other costly improvements.

63. The West Shore of the Quinnipiac Basin and Clinton Park.

The Quinnipiac basin above Grand Avenue is so far shut in by bridges that it can never have a very great commercial value, although it will always be accessible to small craft.

Already the city holds in Clinton Park 1,200 feet of the west shore of this basin and, extending inland from that, it holds also a long narrow strip of parkway. This shore holding might well be extended to include practically all the west shore of the basin as far as Front Street, with a view to maintaining an attractive parklike margin, in connection with which wharves and landings, boathouses and other shore features for small craft can be provided to any extent that may be desirable. The land could be put to no better use under private ownership, and there is every probability that it would be made objectionable by various features that would depreciate the value of residential property and impair the value of the basin to the public.

64. Quinnipiac River East Shore Marshes.

A large portion of the area of salt marsh between the river and the Shore Line Railroad north of Grand Avenue should be acquired by the city for the control of the basin and ultimately for development as a park meadow. There is no pressing need for this acquisition, and the opportunity is not likely to slip away soon, but it should not be lost sight of.

65. Quinnipiac East Shore Quays.

South of Grand Avenue the narrower basin of the river has been more or less developed as a commercial front, chiefly for the use of small boats. The river is relatively narrow here, the highway is crowded close to the bank by the steep hillside, and the water front has been developed in a series of very short, broad wharves and of irregular quays or embankments parallel to the shore. The present developments are not very valuable and do not represent a very effective use of the space. Quinnipiac Avenue ought to be widened sooner or later, and it would seem best for the city to acquire the narrow strip between the street and the river and to plan for a continuous quay. Between the quay and the widened street there would be room for storage yards and for one-story sheds, warehouses, boathouses, etc., over which the river would be visible from the road. Space along the quay could be leased, as with other municipal wharves, except that the water's edge would be kept free for continuous passage in front of the leased yards and shed sites.

66. Fair Haven Parkway.

From Ferry Street bridge eastward there is need for a generous street and pleasure-way, and this can be made by cutting down the rocky ledges between the old bed of the Shore Line

Railroad and the present street. The cost of land takings for such a plan need not be very great and the work of grading can be done when occasion demands it, but unless a definite plan of ample proportions is made before further improvements obstruct the way, this route will either become very bad or will be improved only at great cost.

67. *East Haven Playground.*

Out beyond the rocky ridge of Fair Haven East lies a large swampy area which in time must be drained and reclaimed. Fair Haven Parkway should extend to East Haven, and in conjunction with the parkway a large open field can well be reserved for a playfield where many games of baseball and football may be played in summer and where large areas of shallow water can be formed in winter to provide safe and early skating. Upon this tract a skating pond, even twice as large as the lower Lake Whitney, could be made at slight cost, and this would be so shallow that it would freeze very quickly. Two and one-half miles by road from the Green, this area is but little more remote than Lake Whitney, and it can be reached easily by electric cars.

68. *Branford Parkway.*

The large swampy area south of the village of East Haven has up to the present time made all communication very indirect between New Haven and the charming territory along the shore of the Sound where already many summer homes have been made. To connect these properly with the city, a main artery or a parkway of generous proportions adapted to all kinds of travel, should be laid out.

69. *Morris Cove Parkway.*

Travel to Morris Cove and Fort Hale Park will for a long time follow the narrow routes of Woodward and Townsend avenues, but there will still be need for a quiet and more parklike pleasure approach, such as could be acquired at little expense at the eastern base of the ridge and along which a suitable channel can be made to drain the swamps and marshes toward Lighthouse Point.

SHORE RESERVATIONS.

70. *Fort Hale Park.* (*Area, 49.0 Acres.*)

The city already possesses at Fort Hale Park the strategic point on the east shore where the outer harbor joins the inner harbor. This park of fair size overlooks the long curving shore of Morris Cove and commands fine views across the water toward the city and out to the Sound. In the development of the park the work for a long time to come should be of the simplest kind, and little expense besides that of mere maintenance can be justified. One or two important additions should be made, however, along the eastern boundary and the street leading to the park should be made much wider. Proper connections should be made between this park and the proposed parkway and the public beach at Morris Cove.

71. *Morris Cove Shores.*

The beach of Morris Cove, overlooking the outer harbor and connecting Fort Hale Park with Lighthouse Point, is one of the pleasantest parts of the whole water front. The value of

No. 49. Fort Hale Park from the South. The point of division between the inner and the outer harbors and the probable limit of commercial development on the eastern shores.

No. 50. Morris Cove. A charming spot for private cottages but one in which certain public rights should be secured.

this beach is evidenced by the number of cottages already built facing upon it. It is possible that at the present time a greater amount of enjoyment is obtained from the situation through the presence of these many houses crowded along the edge of the beach, than if the houses were removed and the beach were freely open to the public as a park beach. But as time goes on, as the locality becomes more accessible to the general public and as the character of occupancy is changed, there is danger of increasing encroachments and of the curtailment of public use of the beach upon the one hand, and of an unintelligent and short-sighted exploitation of the public use of it on the other. It would seem important, therefore, to take steps to establish public rights in the beach itself, to prevent further encroachments upon it, and to secure at least occasional vantage points along the bank above it, to be kept permanently open for the use and enjoyment of all.

72. Lighthouse Point.

The low and partly wooded point overlooking the Sound and the harbor is now used in part as a street-railway park and a small point is held by the Government for the lighthouse. Although rather remote, it has a good deal of potential value to the public for recreation purposes, and it should not be allowed to pass into private development of a sort which would jeopardize its ultimate use as a public reservation.

73. Sandy Point.

The marsh land back of Sandy Point, on the west side of the harbor, ought to be obtainable at a very moderate price. Its situation gives it fine views of the inner and outer harbors, and, as West Haven develops, something more than a mere public beach will be desired here as a local public recreation ground.

74. The South Shore.

Public control of the greater part of the south shore frontage in West Haven, overlooking the outer harbor, is much to be desired. Just how much it will pay to acquire, and how to acquire, this shore, will depend upon the attitude of the owners. The greatest value of this shore will always be for public recreation. It has been in part exploited under private control for the sake of the revenue derived from its use by the public, and some of the facilities for public recreation so provided have been worth the price that has been charged, but as a whole this independent development has been very ill-considered. Each exploiter has generally striven to get what he can out of his own particular piece of shore with the least investment, and this has led to the development of shabby, flimsy structures which cover much of the beach, exclude all except paying patrons from the use and enjoyment of the shore, and greatly mar the value of the situation even for the patrons by the character of the development. It should be possible, under a strong central authority, to plan and put through a scheme of development which would greatly increase the recreation value of the beach for the general public, with a corresponding increase in attendance. In connection with such a well-planned development, there would still be plenty of opportunity for private enterprise in catering to the entertainment of the people, but such enterprise would be prevented from doing things as at present that needlessly curtail the total sum of enjoyment to be had from the use of the beach. At Savin Rock we have proposed that the entire rock should be acquired as a picnic ground, and beyond that the bit of rugged shore should be thrown open to the public.

No. 51.   South Shore as it is now being developed for individual exploitation.

OUTER CIRCUIT OF PARKS, PARKWAYS AND RESERVATIONS.

75.   *Savin Rock Marshes.*

The marshy land south of Main Street and east of the existing roadway along the brook is an interesting property of which the value will be greater for public uses than it could be for private development.   This area could well be acquired and treated to overcome the mosquito nuisance and to make the land most useful as proposed for other marsh lands.   It can be developed eventually as a meadow-land park.   Enough of the hill on one or both sides should be acquired to support a border of trees and shrubs about the meadow and to provide for a marginal roadway, with houses facing the park.

76.   *Allingtown Ridge Parkway.*

To connect the Savin Rock marshes with the great reservations forming an outer circuit of the city, a line of parkway should be extended up over Allingtown Ridge to the Maltby Lakes watershed reserve.   This parkway should include one or more widenings on the east, to control the foreground of the view out over the city.   The plan for the parkway crosses the advanced operations of real estate subdivision now spreading over the hilltops, and passes through woods that are fast being swept away to make room for house lots.   Many of the trees can yet be saved and much expense can be avoided if plans are considered and adopted before this development has gone further.

77.   *Allingtown Hill.*

In crossing the hill back of Allingtown the proposed parkway must follow somewhat below the summit.   Above the parkway for some distance there will remain a small strip of land between it and the watershed of the southern Maltby Lakes. A portion of this strip should be acquired for park purposes, as it commands a view of the city and will afford an agreeable outing place for the neighborhood.

78. *Maltby Lakes Watershed.*

The large tract of land which forms the watershed of the Maltby Lakes is largely held by the New Haven Water Company and ought all to be so held for sanitary reasons. It is to be hoped that some arrangement can be made, as proposed above, whereby these areas may be thrown open for public recreation under suitable conditions. This land has many attractive features and it promises to be greatly improved in time with the growth of forests which the water company is now encouraging. The need for opening this reservation to the public may not become urgent for many years to come, but it is worth considering that, when the time does come, the boundaries should include not only the watershed but also such parcels of land as are needed to complete the tract as a landscape reservation and to provide for well-planned boundary streets.

79. *Maltby Ridge Parkway.*

Adjoining the Maltby watershed and following the face of the eastern boundary ridge, a parkway should be provided for in such a way as to continue the proposed Allingtown Ridge Parkway northward on easy lines and grades to the valley of the West River. This parkway should cross the busy cut of Derby Avenue by a bridge at or above the level of the dam of the lower Maltby Lake. Such a bridge will involve the destruction of a few small houses at the south end, where a fill will be required, but will enter the hill on the north in excavation. From the bridge the parkway will cross several large estates which are now held intact, but which may in time be subdivided and be improved by such a parkway. To protect the remarkably fine views over the city from this route the land below it should at several points be acquired, or restricted far enough down the slope to guard against future buildings that would cut off the outlook. Between this proposed parkway and the holdings of the water company, it may prove desirable to acquire all or most of the remaining strip along the top of the ridge.

80 and 81. *Greist's Pond and Hill.*

Another tract of land with a body of water that may in time prove valuable as a public reservation, is that of the shores of the pond on Mr. Greist's property and the hill near the pond overlooking the town. The pond will be desirable for pleasure purposes, and the shores should be held under public control to a moderate distance. The hill will be valuable in connection with the proposed parkway and watershed development.

82. *West River Pond and Parkway.*

Above the mills in Westville there is a tract of river valley, now occupied by small houses, that should be acquired for park purposes. Through this district a broad street is needed from Whalley Avenue to the open valley west of West Rock. The small pond which feeds the mills can well be made much larger by raising the street and increasing the dam. If the pond is so increased there should be a restriction limiting the grade to which it may be drawn down by the mill, as otherwise the basin might be nearly emptied and kept very unsightly during the dry season. The question of raising the pond has already been under consideration, in order to

No. 52. West Rock Park. The area which should be flooded when possession of the south bank
is gained by the City.

increase the skating area and to improve the landscape feature at this end of West Rock. This raise will damage a number of small holdings in the valley, but those properties should first be acquired by the city for street improvements, as suggested in Section 49.

To connect the proposed parkway over Maltby Ridge with West Rock Park and the various routes to the eastward and northward, a pleasure-way should be made, which would cross Whalley Avenue and wind down the steep hill, as indicated on the general plan. Already buildings along Whalley Avenue have encroached upon the most desirable location for such a connection and comparatively early action here seems desirable. After descending the hill the route should connect with the west entrance of West Rock and continue down the valley to the West River Mills Reservation as proposed in Section 46.

No. 53.   West River near Whalley Avenue at Forest Street, where the
proposed lake would terminate.

83.   West Ridge Northward.

The north boundary of West Rock Park should be extended to the northward, to include that part of the ridge now owned by the Poor Farm and all ridge land not held by the water company north to Lake Dawson. This extension should be wide enough also to provide for an ultimate pleasure drive and boundary street up the valley west of the ridge, even though the need for this driveway is rather remote. The proposition on the part of the city to open up a rock quarry in this district is an unfortunate one, as it will mean the removal of a large amount of the talus slope and will expose a raw bank to a great height, making a scar that will remain long after the quarry may be abandoned.

84.   Lake Dawson Watershed.

Far from the city bounds, but not far from the outer limit of suburban development, is a tract of some twenty square miles, consisting of the watershed feeding Lake Dawson, which is practically all owned by the water company. This reservation may in time be made sufficiently accessible to the city to justify some such arrangement between the city and the water company as that suggested for the nearer watersheds.

85. Lake Wintergreen Watershed.

It has been proposed to extend the boundary of West Rock Park northward to the property owned by the water company at Lake Wintergreen and to carry a parkway eastward from there. In that connection a demand may arise for the use of this watershed by the public, calling for a special arrangement for public development.

86. Cherry Hill Parkway.

Across from the north end of West Rock Park, along the foothills to the eastward and through the charming little valley toward Cherry Hill, another parkway is proposed. This would cross the railway near the upper end of Lake Whitney and thus form another unit in the proposed outer circuit. The line of this parkway lies chiefly through farm land, but it is desirable to determine the route and probably to acquire it, at least in part, lest additional buildings along the streets which it crosses interpose serious obstacles. The one point at which any heavy grading will be involved is near Dixwell Avenue, where is will be necessary to cut through the narrow ridge.

87. Lake Whitney Reservation.

Provision should be made for a driveway to extend from the proposed Cherry Hill Parkway along the south shore of Lake Whitney to Whitney Avenue bridge and routes to the eastward. This proposed drive will cross the proposed Winchester Lakes Reservation, but since the Winchester property will probably be kept a long time for its present uses, this route across the north end of it deserves separate and more immediate consideration. The proposed drive falls almost entirely upon lands held by the water company.

Southward from the Whitney Avenue bridge a strip of shore is also needed to provide for a parkway to connect with the bridge to East Rock Park. A considerable portion of the shore belongs to the water company and an amicable arrangement can probably be made with them to provide for putting through such a pleasure-way. This proposition will be somewhat complicated by the possible raising of the level of Lake Whitney, to which contingency the parkway plan should be properly adjusted.

88. Lake Whitney Shores.

The shores of Lake Whitney are largely owned by the water company, but the use of the shores is not so rigidly limited as that of the more distant lakes, for the water in this case is all filtered before it is used. The shores are maintained by the company in an attractive and more or less parklike condition, and the public obtains some enjoyment of them from the adjacent roads and bridges; but still further public use of these shores might well be allowed if the city would undertake the extra burden of maintenance and policing involved thereby.

89. Montowese Parkway.

From the north end of Lake Whitney, in continuation of the proposed outer circuit, a parkway should be extended across the ridge and across the great marshes of the Quinnipiac River to the village of Montowese and the hills beyond. If the parkway along the west shore of Lake Whitney can be developed to sufficient proportions, it may prove better to start a parkway toward

Montowese from the north end of West Rock Park and to cross the marshes at a point farther to the south than that shown, and such a route would have the advantage also of serving better for radial travel from the city toward Montowese; but the best route for crossing the marshes and the Quinnipiac River can be found only after detailed investigation. Some such crossing should be planned for, and at an early date the route through the village should be settled. It would be possible to pass around the village on the south side and thus to avoid some expensive property damages, but such a route will not be so agreeable in many ways as that through the center as shown on the plan.

90. Peter's Rock Reservation.

Back of the village of Montowese, on the route of the proposed outer circuit, the parkway must wind its way up among the hills near Peter's Rock, and there a large area can well be

No. 54. Peter's Rock and the valley east of it where a fine recreation ground can be made.

reserved for public uses of the future. The great rocks should be kept in timber and the valley and open land can be kept clear as playfields. There is no apparent danger of change in the value of this land in the near future; but as it may at any time under private ownership be cut over, quarried into or despoiled in various ways, it should not be neglected while now in a good state of preservation.

91. Foxon Parkway.

From the proposed Peter's Rock Reservation to the eastward a route has been chosen through the rugged hills, where a parkway can be developed upon very fair lines and grades and through a very charming bit of country. This line follows in part the existing country road to Foxon, and near Foxon it is proposed to deepen the cut through the ridge and thence to work down on the east slope and cross the valley of the Farm River to connect with the west slope of the Saltonstall Ridge.

No. 55. Lake Saltonstall. View of the lake from the northeast shore.

No. 56. Saltonstall Watershed, a stony little valley with one of the few great oaks that have so far escaped the axeman. An attractive spot that is now almost inaccessible.

92. *Saltonstall Ridge and Farm River Meadows.*

To connect the proposed Foxon Parkway with the proposed parkway through East Haven and to complete the boundaries of the Lake Saltonstall Reservation, the entire west slope of the ridge should be acquired and in places the proposed taking should extend to the banks of Farm River. Through this track ultimately two lines for pleasure travel should be developed, one along the top of the ridge and one far down the western slope, following in places close to the river through the quiet gentle scenery of the valley.

93. *Lake Saltonstall Watershed.*

The Lake Saltonstall watershed is one of the large tracts of land which the water company has been acquiring to protect the water supply of New Haven. It has been referred to somewhat in detail under the head of "Rural Parks and Reservations" on page 44 of this report. The beautiful scenery of this watershed should in time be made accessible to the public under some such arrangement as there suggested, and it should be developed and managed in conjunction with the proposed parkways and extensions at its boundaries.

No. 57. Lake Saltonstall from the northeast. This charming country is now being
protected from despoliation by the water company.

APPENDIX.

PREFATORY NOTES.

Soon after Mr. Gilbert and Mr. Olmsted began collecting data for their report, Mr. Olmsted wrote the following letter to the Secretary of the Committee, calling for a large amount of statistical information, not available in print and necessary to be collected from a great variety of sources. After some consideration of the questions raised by Mr. Olmsted's letter, the Secretary referred the matter to Professor William Bacon Bailey, and he recommended the employment of Mr. Ronald M. Byrnes, then an academic senior of Yale University, for the work. Mr. Byrnes was consulted and agreed to take up the work, the scope and plan of which may be determined from Mr. Olmsted's letter. Mr. Byrnes was occupied something like three months in preparing the report, in which he embodied material collected from a wide range of sources not readily accessible to the general public. Although the report was used by Mr. Gilbert and Mr. Olmsted in their work, its historical importance as a statistical picture of New Haven at the time at which it was prepared has been considered so great that it has been decided by the Committee to reprint it with some condensations. It is believed that, as time goes on and New Haven grows, Mr. Byrnes's report will be of increasing value and interest to students of the problems connected with the growth and population of American cities. The report follows in Part I of the Appendix.

The recommendations of the Report of the Commission are intended to be general and suggestive rather than definite. But, as an example of such a detailed study of a specific problem as the Report was designed to lead to, it has been thought desirable to include Mr. Olmsted's report on Building Lines in the First Ward—a report secured to assist the members of The Joint Committee of the Civic Federation and the Chamber of Commerce on Streets and Building Lines, in their work of developing public opinion on this important and pressing subject. The services of Mr. Olmsted were enlisted by the Secretary of the Mayor's Committee and paid for by the Chairman of the Committee on Buildings, Streets and Shade Trees of the Civic Federation. This additional report is therefore included in the Appendix, Part II.

GEORGE DUDLEY SEYMOUR.

APPENDIX—PART I.

STATISTICAL REPORT ON THE CITY OF NEW HAVEN.

Brookline, Mass., 26th October, 1907.

Mr. George Dudley Seymour,
    868 Chapel Street, New Haven, Conn.

My Dear Mr. Seymour:

As I mentioned to you yesterday it seems to me that it would help to a clearer framing of the problem on which your committee wants advice and suggestion from Mr. Gilbert and me, to gather and digest a considerable amount of such statistics as are available in regard to the economic and social conditions and tendencies of the city.

Mr. Gilbert and I have no special training or professional skill as municipal diagnosticians, to discover what sort of things now lacking to the city would contribute most to the satisfaction of its citizens; our professional training and experience put us in no better position than any other intelligent observers to advise New Haven *what to do*; it is only for devising *how to do it* that we are professionally equipped. We shall be glad to take such part as we can with you and the other members of your committee in making a diagnosis of the needs of the community, and so far as concerns observation of the physical conditions of the city we can quickly get hold of the more essential facts; but the human facts are just as important and much more tedious to collate.

I suppose in its broadest statement the question that your committee puts before itself is something like this: in addition to what would be accomplished in any case through the normal or routine operations of municipal government, what can reasonably be done to increase the physical convenience and agreeableness of New Haven as a place for its population to live and work in?

To answer this question in a wise and farsighted way involves a careful forecast of the size, character and needs of the future population; for the immediate effect of any large permanent improvements is of slight importance compared with their cumulative effect on successive later generations. In regard to the formation of parks and other permanent open spaces, and especially in regard to the layout of thoroughfares and the transportation system, the probable future distribution and requirements of the population should absolutely control present decisions. Light should be sought wherever it can be found on the subject of existing conditions and tendencies of growth and change in the population; as to numbers, distribution, occupation, character, habits of life, needs and economic resources. After all is gathered that can be it will cast a very feeble and uncertain illumination on the future, but if it is intelligently used it is a good deal better than guessing or going it blind. Statistics showing the rate and manner of changes during the last few decades can readily be secured for certain comparable kinds of facts, some of which may be suggested by the following headings. Different kinds of facts are obtainable in different cities, and you will have to take what can be got without too much special investigation or clerical labor. So far as possible it is desirable to get the figures by districts, i. e., by wards, school districts, etc., as well as by totals for the whole city, and when this is done watch must be kept for change of boundaries between successive records.

Population, total and by classes: e. g., voters or poll taxpayers, other taxpayers, children of school age, children attending public schools, children attending parochial schools, university students, dependents (insane and criminal), foreign born.

Taxable valuation of land, of buildings, of personal property.

Tax rate and total levy.

City debt.

Industrial establishments: statistics of employees, etc.

Freight shipments inward and outward.

Railroad passengers per annum.

Street railway passengers per annum.

Present routes of street car lines and number of passengers carried on each route, either on typical day or average. (This ought to throw some light on the question of congestion of traffic and where and how to seek relief. It would be well to look out for the disturbing influence of football games on these figures.)

Counts of vehicular traffic, if such have ever been made in connection with choice of pavement materials or other street problems.

Facts, statistical or otherwise, in regard to housing conditions and rentals, and tendencies therein.

Death rate (by causes, by districts, and by ages if accessible). Other vital statistics of Board of Health.

Miles of street, paved and unpaved, at different periods.

Miles of street railway track (single and double).

Areas of districts used in tabulating population statistics.

Percentage of these areas occupied: by streets and squares, by railroad property, by parks and public grounds, by cemeteries, by water and marshes.

Area of the several school grounds and buildings.

It is needless to say that in compiling information of matters of this sort precision of detail is of far less consequence than watchfulness against discrepancies in the method by which supposedly comparable data are derived and against gross omissions.

Hoping that these suggestions will not seem to open a vaster prospect of statistical labor than I really have in mind, I remain,

Respectfully yours,

FREDERICK LAW OLMSTED.

REPORT AS COMPILED BY RONALD M. BYRNES.

As regards the nature of the material which I have attempted to collect; I have followed Mr. Olmsted's suggestions almost literally and have limited my research to such statistics as would, in my estimation, contribute to "a careful forecast of the size, character and needs of the future population." In no case do the figures run back previous to 1850, and in most cases it has been impossible to obtain reliable figures previous to 1870. Moreover, the figures for 1880 and before are not comparable with the later figures, because all the ward lines were changed in 1881 and consequently the wards of the present time do not correspond with those of 1880 and before, and the city, or rather town as a whole, has changed in size, by the addition of Westville and Fair Haven East, which now compose the Thirteenth, the Fourteenth and the Fifteenth wards, respectively, of the city and town of New Haven.

In presenting the material which I have collected, I shall first give the figures for the city as a whole and after determining the general trend of the social and economic conditions of the city entire, I shall take up the individual wards and determine the trend in each of these arbitrary subdivisions.

GENERAL SOCIAL AND ECONOMIC CONDITIONS.

The following table shows the total population of the city of New Haven, in the census years since 1850, and the population distinguished as white and colored, native and foreign:

TABLE I

POPULATION IN CENSUS YEARS SINCE 1850*

Year	Total	White	Colored	Native	Foreign
1850	20,338	19,356	989	16,641	3,697
1860	39,267	37,779	1,488	28,622	10,645
1870	50,840	49,090	1,749	36,484	14,346
1880	62,882	60,648	2,192	47,214	15,668
1890	81,298	78,795	2,503	58,304	22,994
1900	108,027	105,038	2,989	77,225	30,802

* These figures have been plotted in diagrams No. 1, page 14 and No. 2, page 15.

By this table we see that New Haven's population has increased more than fivefold in fifty years, truly an amazing growth. The following table shows the per cent. increase from decade to decade:

TABLE I a

PERCENTILE INCREASE OF TOTAL POPULATION

1850–1860	93.4%	1870–1880	23.7%
1860–1870	29.4	1880–1890	29.2
	1890–1900	32.8 (or 24.8 for same area as above).	

From this we see that the greatest relative increase was from 1850-1860, when the population almost doubled itself. The slower rate of increase from 1870-1880 is probably the result of a falling-off of the birth rate following the Civil War. The seeming acceleration from 1890 to 1900 is not really just, inasmuch as the figures for Westville and Fair Haven East are included in the total for 1900, but not in the total for 1890. Subtract the population of these two districts (comprising the Thirteenth, Fourteenth, and Fifteenth wards) and the figures for 1900 would read, 101,512 and the per cent. increase would be for 1880-1890, 29.2 per cent., and for 1890-1900, 24.8 per cent. These three wards increased from 4,747 in 1890 to 6,515 in 1900, giving an increase of 37.2 per cent. Taking it in another way, by adding in the population of these three wards in 1890, we find that the present city of New Haven increased from 86,045 in 1890 to 108,027 in 1900; a percentile increase of 25.5 per cent.

Looking again at Table I, we see that the white population has increased somewhat more than fivefold, and the colored population has increased only a little more than threefold. The native born population of New Haven has multiplied about four and one-half times while the foreign born has increased more than eightfold. The percentile increase of the foreign born by decades is as follows:

TABLE I b

PERCENTILE INCREASE OF FOREIGN BORN

1850–1860	187.9%	1880–1890	46.7%
1860–1870	34.6	1890–1900	33.9
1870–1880	9.2		

This table shows how irregular has been the increase of foreign born population of New Haven, due to the fact that the increase had to come, of course, from immigration and not from reproduction. It will be interesting to find out the proportion that the colored and foreign born bear to the whole population at the various periods.

TABLE I c

PERCENTAGE OF TOTAL POPULATION

Year	Colored	Foreign Born	Year	Colored	Foreign Born
1850	4.8%	13.4%	1880	3.4%	24.9%
1860	3.7	27.1	1890	3.0	28.2
1870	3.4	28.2	1900	2.7	28.5

Here we see that the colored have not kept pace with the total increase, while the proportion of foreign born in the city has increased very materially and at the next census will probably have reached 30 per cent. or more of the total population.

The next question is, what is the character, what are the chief nationalities, of the foreign born population of New Haven? This question is answered by the following table:

TABLE II*

DISTRIBUTION OF FOREIGN BORN BY PRINCIPAL NATIONALITIES

Year	Irish	English and Scotch	German and Swede	Italian	Russian	All Others
1860	7,391	....	1,842	....	....	1,412
1870	9,601	1,087	2,423	....	....	1,235
1880	9,630	1,358	2,802	102	....	1,776
1890	10,574	1,658	5,314	1,876	1,160	2,412
1900	10,491	1,912	6,119	5,262	3,193	3,825

* This table has been plotted in diagram No. 2, page 15.

Here we see the Irish overwhelmingly in the lead at the earliest period, with only the Germans as any considerable additional factor in the foreign born population. But it is noteworthy that the Irish have not been greatly recruited while the Germans and Swedes have increased more than threefold. Another remarkable feature is the rapid increase of the Italian and Russian contingents. Both were practically negligible quantities in 1880; within twenty years the Italians increased to over 5,000, and the Russians to over 3,000; together forming nearly one-third of the total foreign born population. If figures were accessible to date, I do not hesitate to say that we should probably find the Italians and Russians forming practically one-half of the total foreign born population of New Haven.

Table IIa shows the percentage of each considerable nationality represented, in the years designated, to the total foreign born population.

TABLE II a

PERCENTAGE OF TOTAL FOREIGN BORN

Year	Irish	English and Scotch	German and Swede	Italian	Russian	All Others
1860	69.4%	..	17.3%	..	..	13.3%
1870	66.0	7.5%	16.9	..	..	8.7
1880	61.4	8.6	17.9	0.6%	..	11.3
1890	44.0	7.2	23.1	8.1	4.9%	12.4
1900	30.4	6.2	19.8	17.1	13.7	12.4

In accordance with Mr. Olmsted's request, I have also obtained the number of voters, of poll taxpayers and the total number of taxpayers, as far back toward 1850 as there were records available for each class. The statistics of the number of voters are probably somewhat inaccurate, since the only records available, as far as I could ascertain, were the summaries and vouchers deposited with the city clerk at each election, and inasmuch as the elections were sometimes for different purposes, the number of voters would naturally vary with the importance of the purpose. That is, more voters are apt to be "made" before an important election than before one of relative unimportance. Moreover, in some of the years the voucher for a ward or two, perhaps, would be missing, because these vouchers are not required to be kept on file and, indeed, have been relegated to the dust of the City Hall attic, where they reposed in an almost hopeless jumble.

TABLE III

VOTERS AND TAXPAYERS SINCE 1850

Year	Voters	Poll Taxpayers	Total Taxpayers	Year	Voters	Poll Taxpayers	Total Taxpayers
1850	.....	2,893	.....	1900	22,807	2,418	12,307
1860	.....	5,695	.....	1901	24,929	2,297	12,169
1870	.....	4,530	.....	1902	24,319	2,304	12,230
1880	.....	2,630	.....	1903	24,240	2,228	12,370
1890	18,835	2,365	.....	1904	26,736	2,345	12,482
1895	18,589	2,501	11,392	1905	26,290	2,403	12,886
1898	22,653	2,512	12,087	1906	25,211	2,563	13,182
1899	23,232	2,439	12,211	1907	24,796	.....	....

These figures should be valuable for finding the proportion they bear to the total population as enumerated in the censal years and these proportions may be used as an aid in estimating the population in the intercensal years. The number of children of school age, or the number of children attending school, is another basis in general use for estimating intercensal populations. Table IV gives these figures as far as obtainable. The first column shows the number of children between the ages of five and sixteen years, as obtained by the census taken each year by the Board of Education. The figures for 1890 and on are actually for the October of the preceding year in each case; since the school census is taken in October, and there is less error in using the figures for the latter end of the preceding year than those for the latter end of the current year. The same explanation applies also to the second column, the number of children attending school, as published yearly in the report of the Board of Education. The third column gives the number of persons between the ages of five and twenty years, as enumerated by the United States Census in 1890 and 1900.

TABLE IV

SCHOOL CHILDREN

Year	Children of School Age	Children Attending School	Children between 5 and 20 years	Year	Children of School Age	Children Attending School	Children between 5 and 20 years
1870	10,477	.....	.....	1901	23,301	19,569	....
1880	13,897	.....	.....	1902	23,830	19,912	....
1890	18,314	14,609	24,411	1903	24,746	20,638	....
1895	19,787	16,096	.....	1904	24,903	21,375	....
1898	21,648	18,006	.....	1905	25,047	21,909	....
1899	22,220	18,460	. ...	1906	26,114	22,476	....
1900	22,741	19,020	30,746	1907	27,015	22,937	....

A question not suggested by Mr. Olmsted, but which, it seems to me, might be of interest, relates to the number of houses, i.e., dwellings, in New Haven at various periods and to the average number of persons to a dwelling. The following table answers the question:

TABLE V

DWELLINGS

Year	Number of Dwellings	Persons per Dwelling	Year	Number of Dwellings	Persons per Dwelling
1870	8,100	6.28	1890	11,194	7.26
1880	9,961	6.31	1900	15,240	7.10

Of course this table shows absolutely nothing as to the housing conditions in New Haven. The increase in the average number of persons per dwelling might come quite as well, and probably does, from an increase in the average size of dwelling, as from any congestion.

The only available sources of birth and death statistics in New Haven are the City and State Boards of Health, and their figures do not antedate 1880.

Each year the State Board of Health publishes the total number of births during the year and computes a birth rate on the basis of an estimated population. Table VI gives the number of births and the estimated birth rate for each year in question since 1880.

TABLE VI

BIRTHS AND BIRTH RATES

Year	Births	Rate	Year	Births	Rate
1880	1,742	27.7	1901	2,794	26.4
1890	2,433	28.2	1902	2,930	25.8
1895	2,778	27.7	1903	2,952	26.0
1898	2,975	26.1	1904	3,127	25.7
1899	2,891	26.5	1905	3,135	26.8
1900	2,855	24.9			

The following table gives the total number of births in New Haven per annum for the designated years; and the number of white births, of colored births, of births from native parents, and births from parents at least one of whom is foreign:

TABLE VI a

NATIVITY OF BIRTHS

Year	Total	White	Colored	Native	Foreign
1880	1,742	1,691	51	538	1,204
1890	2,433	2,402	31	738	1,695
1895	2,778	2,708	70	1,049	1,729
1898	2,975	2,894	81	1,059	1,916
1899	2,891	2,818	73	1,032	1,859
1900	2,855	....	..	1,048	1,807
1901	2,793	....	..	966	1,827
1902	2,930	....	..	991	1,939
1903	2,952	....	..	993	1,969
1904	3,127	....	..	1,018	2,109
1905	3,135	....	..	999	2,136

These figures are of no use except as showing the absolute increase in the number of births for the whole population and for its several subdivisions. The following table gives the crude birth rate, i.e., the number of births per 1,000 population, in the censal years since 1880, there being no basis for such rates in the intercensal years:

TABLE VI b

NATIVITY BIRTH RATES

Year	Total	White	Colored	Native	Foreign
1880	27.7	27.8	23.2	11.3	76.8
1890	28.2	30.4	12.3	12.6	73.7
1900	24.9	....	....	13.5	58.6

This table shows a quite perceptible decline in the birth rate for the entire city from 1890 to 1900. The great discrepancy between the rates for the native born and the foreign is due to two reasons. First, the foreign births include all births from parents only one of whom is foreign, and thus natives who marry foreigners are not credited in the column of native births, although included among the native population. Thus the crude native birth rate, as reckoned above, is unfairly low and the foreign is unfairly high. Secondly, the foreign population is nearly all in the reproducing ages; that is, there is nowhere near as large a proportion of children and of men and women over fifty years of age among the foreign born as there is among the native. This, of course, would increase the former's birth rate. To eliminate the first cause of error, I have subtracted each year from the total number of foreign births as given in Table VI the number of births from parents only one of whom is foreign. The result is given below:

TABLE VI c

NATIVITY OF BIRTHS AND BIRTH RATES CORRECTED FOR PARENTAGE

Year	BIRTHS		Year	BIRTH RATES	
	Native	Foreign		Native	Foreign
1880	538	960	1880	11.3	61.2
1890	738	1,352	1890	12.6	58.7
1900	1,048	1,436	1900	13.5	46.6

Two things are noticeable here; first, that the native rate seems to be gradually rising, and secondly, that the foreign rate is consistently diminishing. The second fact is probably the result of the gradual acquisition by the foreign born of a larger juvenile and senile population.

The next consideration is the number of births furnished each year by each principal nationality represented among the foreign born. This information is given in the table below:

TABLE VII

BIRTHS FROM FOREIGN BORN PARENTS, CLASSED BY NATIONALITIES

Year	Irish	English and Scotch	German and Swede	Italian	Russian	Year	Irish	English and Scotch	German and Swede	Italian	Russian
1880	439	36	112	...	...	1901	289	28	184	545	223
1890	305	45	241	145	96	1902	275	30	171	670	222
1895	331	46	280	288	247	1903	263	18	159	753	209
1898	357	37	213	408	274	1904	248	18	152	828	252
1899	310	42	199	469	256	1905	220	18	137	861	332
1900	301	21	194	512	223						

The salient features of the preceding table are, first, the steady decrease in the number of Irish and German births, although the Irish and German populations have increased in numbers since 1880; second, the remarkable increase and large number of Italian and Russian births, which together in 1905 formed more than one-half of the births from foreign born parents, and more than one-third of the total number of births in New Haven. The following table of birth rates for the censal year brings out still more clearly the foregoing facts:

TABLE VII a

BIRTH RATES OF FOREIGN BORN BY NATIONALITIES

Year	Irish	English and Scotch	German and Swede	Italian	Russian
1880	45.5	26.5	39.9	...	...
1890	28.8	27.1	45.3	77.2	82.7
1900	28.7	11.0	31.7	97.3	69.7

When we consider that a crude birth rate of 30 per 1,000 is a large one, it can readily be seen that the foreign born population of New Haven is doing considerably more than its share of the city's reproducing.

The following death figures are also compiled from the reports of the City and State Boards of Health. A high birth rate accompanied by a high death rate is of no advantage to a community; it is far better to have a low birth rate and a low death rate, and in many cases a high birth rate is largely offset by a high infantile mortality.

TABLE VIII

DEATHS AND DEATH RATES

Year	Deaths	Rate	Year	Deaths	Rate
1880	1,121	17.8	1901	1,974	17.9
1890	1,742	21.4	1902	1,869	16.6
1895	1,890	20.1	1903	1,941	16.9
1898	1,843	17.9	1904	2,016	17.2
1899	1,717	16.2	1905	2,227	18.7
1900	1,963	18.1	1906	2,321	19.2

This table corresponds with Table VI of the births; that is, it gives the total number of deaths in New Haven per annum, for each year in question since 1880, and the death rate for each year on the basis of the estimated intercensal populations.

TABLE VIII a

NUMBER OF DEATHS IN NEW HAVEN

Year	Total	Native	Foreign	Year	Total	Native	Foreign
1880	1,121	831	290	1901	1,974	1,339	635
1890	1,742	1,216	526	1902	1,869	1,267	602
1895	1,890	606	1,284	1903	1,941	1,306	635
1898	1,843	1,288	555	1904	2,016	1,377	639
1899	1,717	1,144	573	1905	2,227	1,199	1,028
1900	1,963	1,357	606	1906	2,321	1,579	742

Absolute numbers like these cannot afford any basis for comparison; wherefore the following table giving the crude death rates, i.e., the number of deaths per 1,000 population, in the censal years 1880, 1890 and 1900:

TABLE VIII b

DEATH RATES

Year	Total	Native	Foreign
1880	17.8	17.6	18.6
1890	21.4	20.8	22.9
1900	18.1	13.9	19.6

Here we see the death rate among the foreign born exceeding that among the native in every instance. Comparing the totals in this table with the totals in Table VIa we obtain the following:

TABLE VIII c

EXCESS OF BIRTH RATES OVER DEATH RATES

Year	Death Rate	Birth Rate	Excess
1880	17.8	27.7	9.9
1890	21.4	28.2	6.8
1900	18.1	24.9	6.9

This shows that the annual increase in population through births alone would average little more than 7 per 1,000, or 0.7 per cent., and that a large proportion of the growth in population shown in Table I must have been through recruits from beyond the city limits.

Taking up now the principal nationalities represented among the foreign born population of New Haven, let us see how many deaths each nationality contributes per annum.

TABLE IX

DEATHS OF FOREIGN BORN BY NATIONALITIES

Year	Irish	English and Scotch	German and Swede	Italian	Russian	Year	Irish	English and Scotch	German and Swede	Italian	Russian
1880	202	22	25	..	..	1901	302	65	124	50	27
1890	303	43	66	20	..	1902	296	44	107	64	30
1895	497	74	*177	95	56	1903	300	61	98	68	22
1898	284	49	89	56	21	1904	291	58	119	77	29
1899	291	52	112	41	20	1905	320	65	125	91	49
1900	306	49	133	57	18	1906	326	55	134	107	48

* The Swedes are not reckoned in with the Germans previous to 1895.

Several deductions may be made from the foregoing figures, but for comparison the following table of death rates is much more useful:

TABLE IX a

DEATH RATES OF FOREIGN BORN BY NATIONALITIES

Year	Irish	English and Scotch	German and Swede	Italian	Russian
1880	20.9	16.2	8.9	...	...
1890	28.6	25.9	12.4	10.6	...
1900	29.1	25.6	21.7	10.8	5.6

A detailed comparison of this table with Table·VIIa is very illumining. The margin of births over deaths for the Irish was nearly 25 per 1,000 population in 1880; in 1890 it had decreased to 0.2 per 1,000, and in 1900 it became a minus 0.4. The same thing is true of the English and Scotch, only in an even more marked degree. Another noticeable feature is the very low death rates of the Italians and Russians in comparison with their very high birth rates; two facts, which taken together point to the probability of a very large proportion of these nationalities being in the middle-age groups.

I have already said that a high birth rate may be offset by a high death rate; and it has been generally agreed that a high infantile mortality is to be regarded as an unmitigated evil for a community, even though a high birth rate allows for an increase of population.

TABLE X

INFANTILE MORTALITY

Year	Deaths under one year of age	Mortality Rate per 1000 Births	Year	Deaths under one year of age	Mortality Rate per 1000 Births
1890	340	111.5	1901	387	138.5
1895	437	157.3	1902	406	138.5
1898	417	140.1	1903	385	130.4
1899	316	108.1	1904	399	127.6
1900	452	158.2	1905	432	137.8

When we consider that England is dismayed by her infant mortality of 132 per 1,000 during the past year, we can realize how serious New Haven's infant mortality has been in the majority of years since 1890.

Another subject on which Mr. Olmsted desired information was the number of deaths per annum, classified by principal causes of death. The following table gives this information for the years since 1880:

TABLE XI

DEATHS CLASSIFIED BY PRINCIPAL CAUSES

	1880	1890	1895	1898	1899	1900	1901	1902	1903	1904	1905	1906
Consumption	165	230	210	225	202	203	220	214	186	195	183	196
Pneumonia	62	222	178	182	151	223	191	161	232	213	240	302
Heart Disease	47	106	145	102	190	184	176	176	177	189	233	222
Violence	45	72	83	71	80	95	97	123	122	146	112	132
Diarrheal Disease	63	133	178	161	117	182	171	208	149	141	178	170
Bright's Disease	...	...	82	109	111	107	115	101	98	140	122	135
Apoplexy	20	61	76	78	90	82	98	116	101	98	119	129
Cancer	37	39	72	71	74	71	98	87	90	81	110	98
Bronchitis	45	76	105	82	61	92	53	64	61	51	57	68
Old Age	38	53	45	32	61	52	48	33	46	43	56	66
Meningitis	49	55	57	40	41	34	44	42	51	41	44	40
Typhoid	15	24	34	39	28	26	103	39	42	33	49	63
Convulsions	47	45	55	42	51	56	36	33	28	26	...	...
Whooping Cough	21	19	34	..	..	21	..	34	23	14	8	36
Diphtheria and Croup	73	106	27	36	22	18	25	10	19	16	15	47
Scarlet Fever	...	...	...	...	...	7	...	8	15	6	7	...
Cerebro Spinal Meningitis	...	...	...	...	...	...	...	...	...	...	104	9

For comparison with the above I have subjoined the figures for the number of cases of (not deaths from) the three principal contagious diseases.

TABLE XI a

CASES OF CONTAGIOUS DISEASES

Year	Diphtheria	Scarlet Fever	Typhoid	Total	Year	Diphtheria	Scarlet Fever	Typhoid	Total
1890	304	98	120	522	1902	124	305	183	612
1895	108	149	102	259	1903	137	218	180	535
1898	176	68	177	321	1904	146	164	166	476
1899	153	109	147	409	1905	92	185	247	534
1900	119	174	110	403	1906	318	126	265	709
1901	190	169	696	1,155					

The only topics left to consider are the various ones relative to the area and financial condition of the city. The total area of the city and town of New Haven, as estimated by the city engineer expressly for this report, is given below; together with the area of the town in the harbor, and the area of all the parks in the respective sections of the town. By the "Annex" (see below) is meant Fair Haven East, that is, the Fourteenth and Fifteenth wards.

TABLE XII

AREA OF THE TOWN OF NEW HAVEN IN ACRES

	Total	Parks	Harbor	Land
City (and Harbor)	6,291	290.38	936	5,355
Westville	3,058	252.68	....	3,058
Annex	4,785	66.02	1,579	3,047
Harbor south of city and west of Annex	206	....	206	....
Annex in Quinnipiac River	....	....	159	....
	14,340	609.08	2,880	11,460

The area of the town by wards is given below; the figures do not include the area of any of the wards in the harbor. The Fourteenth and Fifteenth wards are given together, as I have no estimates for them separately.

TABLE XIII

AREA OF THE TOWN BY WARDS IN ACRES

First Ward	176	Eighth Ward	485
Second Ward	547	Ninth Ward	1,034
Third Ward	322	Tenth Ward	602
Fourth Ward	514	Eleventh Ward	303
Fifth Ward	232	Twelfth Ward	819
Sixth Ward	167	Thirteenth Ward	3,058
Seventh Ward	154	Fourteenth and Fifteenth Wards	3,047

Of course, these figures are of use as far back as 1890, since the present ward lines took shape in 1881. The density of population in the various wards can be found for 1890 and 1900 by combining the preceding table with the following:

TABLE XIII a

POPULATION OF NEW HAVEN BY WARDS

	1890	1900		1890	1900
First Ward	4,928	4,850	Ninth Ward	8,451	11,427
Second Ward	6,227	8,134	Tenth Ward	5,754	7,823
Third Ward	9,714	12,367	Eleventh Ward	4,850	5,520
Fourth Ward	10,525	13,751	Twelfth Ward	6,470	9,228
Fifth Ward	4,174	4,768	Thirteenth Ward	1,975	2,695
Sixth Ward	5,691	6,250	Fourteenth Ward	1,696	1,851
Seventh Ward	8,594	9,504	Fifteenth Ward	1,076	1,969
Eighth Ward	5,920	7,620			

As regards the mileage of paved and unpaved streets at various periods, the following estimates have been prepared for this report by the city engineer, on the basis that there are now in the first twelve wards a total of 155 miles of street and that the total mileage of street in these wards has not greatly changed since 1850. It is estimated, in addition, that in the Thirteenth, Fourteenth and Fifteenth wards there is a total of fifty miles of street, twenty-two miles of which are paved.

TABLE XIV

MILEAGE OF STREETS IN FIRST TWELVE WARDS

Year	Paved	Unpaved	Year	Paved	Unpaved
1850	5.000	145.000	1900	49.966	103.034
1860	5.000	145.000	1901	52.951	97.049
1870	7.000	143.000	1902	53.831	96.169
1880	13.476	136.524	1903	54.994	95.006
1890	33.479	116.521	1904	54.994	95.006
1895	40.225	109.775	1905	54.994	95.006
1898	42.632	107.368	1906	55.441	94.559
1899	44.008	105.992			

The total mileage of street railway track in New Haven, figured as a single track, was 72.29 miles in 1895, 79.93 in 1900, and 131.76 miles, including the annexation, in 1907. The total number of passengers carried during the year 1907 was 31,599,353. The approximate number of passengers carried on the principal routes during the month of December, 1907, was as follows:

STREET CAR TRAVEL FOR DECEMBER, 1907

	Total	Per Day
Fair Haven-Shelton Avenue	225,560	7,276
Fair Haven-Westville	221,213	7,136
Dixwell Avenue-Railroad Station	174,330	5,623
Country Club-Savin Rock	231,894	7,480
State and Ferry-Savin Rock	284,615	9,181
Schuetzen Park	228,620	7,375

The taxable valuation of real estate in New Haven has increased enormously in the last fifty years, and the valuation of personal property has more than doubled. Table XV shows the valuation of real estate and personal property since 1860, together with the tax rate (in mills) for the respective years.

TABLE XV

TAXABLE VALUATION OF PROPERTY

Year	Real Estate	Personal Property	Tax Rate	Year	Real Estate	Personal Property	Tax Rate
1860	$15,855,338	$ 9,883,463	18¼	1900	$99,456,032	$16,242,775	13¼
1870	31,547,275	16,926,802	19½	1901	92,599,947	11,956,076	12¾
1880	34,797,569	13,097,158	17¹⁄₁₀	1902	94,547,359	11,076,209	13¼
1890	40,669,983	11,501,148	19½	1903	94,061,580	13,151,531	13¼
1895	45,529,140	12,525,303	21	1904	95,142,885	14,119,932	13¼
1898	53,680,489	13,435,793	18	1905	98,146,457	12,653,305	14
1899	53,856,511	13,366,064	21	1906	100,412,373	12,631,922	13½

These figures show a general increase in the valuation of real estate, but the figures for personal property in recent years seem very low in comparison.

There still remains for consideration the debt of the city of New Haven. The figures for this are given below:

TABLE XVI

CITY DEBT

Year	Total Bonded Debt	Floating Debt	Year	Total Bonded Debt	Floating Debt
1860	$ 100,000	$ 56,000	1901	$3,429,500	$455,000
1870	214,000	.....	1902	3,297,500	350,000
1880	829,000	25,000	1903	3,337,500	275,000
1890	1,274,000	.....	1904	3,297,500	299,000
1895	1,210,000	87,336	1905	3,636,500	50,000
1898	2,933,200	571,029	1906	3,524,000	.....
1900	3,757,000	200,000			

These figures show very considerable increases up to 1900, with an actual decrease since that date.

WARD STATISTICS.

Having ended the presentation of the statistical material which I have collected to show the "economic and social condition" of the city entire, I shall take up the wards individually and present such similar statistics for these arbitrary subdivisions as were obtainable. Unfortunately, the records are far more incomplete for the wards than they are for the city entire. Moreover, since the present ward lines have existed only since 1881, it would be futile to introduce any figures previous to 1890 and to compare them with the later ward figures. Tables XVII and XVIII, immediately following, are merely preliminary ones, showing the ranking of the wards in size and population.

TABLE XVII

WARDS RANKED ACCORDING TO SIZE

		Acres			Acres
1	Thirteenth Ward	3,058	8	Eighth Ward	485
2	Fourteenth and Fifteenth Wards	3,047	9	Third Ward	322
3	Ninth Ward	1,034	10	Eleventh Ward	303
4	Twelfth Ward	819	11	Fifth Ward	232
5	Tenth Ward	602	12	First Ward	176
6	Second Ward	547	13	Sixth Ward	167
7	Fourth Ward	514	14	Seventh Ward	154

TABLE XVIII

WARDS RANKED BY POPULATION

		1890			1900
1	Fourth Ward	10,525	1	Fourth Ward	13,751
2	Third Ward	9,714	2	Third Ward	12,367
3	Seventh Ward	8,594	3	Ninth Ward	11,427
4	Ninth Ward	8,451	4	Seventh Ward	9,504
5	Twelfth Ward	6,470	5	Twelfth Ward	9,228
6	Second Ward	6,227	6	Second Ward	8,134
7	Eighth Ward	5,920	7	Tenth Ward	7,823
8	Tenth Ward	5,754	8	Eighth Ward	7,620
9	Sixth Ward	5,691	9	Sixth Ward	6,250
10	First Ward	4,928	10	Eleventh Ward	5,520
11	Eleventh Ward	4,850	11	First Ward	4,850
12	Fifth Ward	4,174	12	Fifth Ward	4,758
13	Thirteenth Ward	1,975	13	Thirteenth Ward	2,695
14	Fourteenth Ward	1,696	14	Fifteenth Ward	1,969
15	Fifteenth Ward	1,076	15	Fourteenth Ward	1,851

FIRST WARD.

The First Ward, situated in the heart of the city, ranks twelfth among the wards in size, and the population ranked tenth in 1890 and eleventh in 1900. Its area is 176 acres. Table I gives its population statistics.

TABLE I
POPULATION

Year	Total	White	Colored	Native	Foreign
1890	4,928	4,814	114	3,928	970
1900	4,850	4,764	86	3,942	908

Here we see that the total population of the ward actually decreased 1.5 per cent. during these ten years, and that the native element of the population was the only one which increased. Table II gives the proportion of the colored and foreign elements to the total population.

TABLE II
PERCENTAGE OF TOTAL POPULATION

Year	Colored	Foreign
1890	2.3%	19.6%
1900	1.7	18.7

The density of the population in this ward was 28.0 per acre in 1890, and 27.5 per acre in 1900.

In 1890 there were 635 dwellings in the First Ward, with an average number of 7.7 persons per dwelling; in 1900 the dwellings had decreased to 578, with an average number of 8.39 persons per dwelling. The number of voters in the First Ward is given below:

TABLE III
RECORD OF VOTERS

1890 1,065	1900 1,058	1904 1,043
1895 948	1901 1,023	1905 1,002
1898 938	1902 888	1906 892
1899 985	1903 901	1907 811

The number of children between five and twenty years of age was 1,306 in 1890, and 1,174 in 1900.

No record is kept of births by wards, so that it is impossible to compute a birth rate. The number of deaths and the death rates for the First Ward are given below:

TABLE IV
DEATHS AND DEATH RATE

Year	Deaths	Death Rate	Year	Deaths	Death Rate
1890	68	12.10	1902	33	6.70
1895	46	7.66	1903	38	7.90
1898	48	8.00	1904	34	7.00
1899	45	7.50	1905	34	7.00
1900	56	11.00	1906	49	9.00
1901	56	11.00			

Of course it is understood that these death rates are based on estimated intercensal populations, since there is no enumeration in New Haven from one census to the next. The vital statistics of the First Ward are completed by Table V, which shows the number of cases of the principal contagious diseases which have been reported within the ward's borders since 1890.

TABLE V
CASES OF CONTAGIOUS DISEASES

Year	Diphtheria	Scarlet Fever	Typhoid	Total	Year	Diphtheria	Scarlet Fever	Typhoid	Total
1890	3	5	1	9	1902	3	5	6	14
1895	3	3	3	14	1903	1		10	11
1898	6	3	7	16	1904	4	6	5	15
1899	1	4	7	12	1905	1	3	7	11
1900	3	2	9	14	1906	1	8	10	19
1901	7	4	36	47					

The total park area of the First Ward is 16.05 acres. The total floor space of the only public school in the ward aggregates 33,180 square feet, and the space available for school playground is 11,500 square feet.

SECOND WARD.

The Second Ward ranks sixth among the wards in area, and in population also ranked sixth both in 1890 and 1900. Its area is 547 acres, of which only .36 of an acre is devoted to park purposes. In this ward lies the two large cemeteries, Evergreen and Maple Dale. Its population statistics are as follows:

TABLE I
POPULATION

Year	Total	White	Colored	Native	Foreign
1890	6,227	6,080	147	4,611	1,616
1900	8,134	7,907	227	6,016	2,118

In this ward we find the population to have increased during the ten years as follows: Total, 30.6 per cent.; Native, 30.4 per cent.; Foreign, 31.0 per cent.; White, 30.0 per cent.; Colored, 54.4 per cent.

The foreign born have increased slightly more rapidly in numbers than the native, while the colored have increased proportionately much faster than the white. The following table, however, shows that there is at present no danger of this ward becoming predominantly negro. The figures show the proportion of colored and foreign elements to the total population of the ward.

TABLE II
PERCENTAGE OF TOTAL POPULATION

Year	Colored	Foreign
1890	2.3%	25.9%
1900	2.7	26.0

The density of population of this ward was 11.3 per acre in 1890, and 14.8 per acre in 1900. In 1890 there were 999 dwellings in the Second Ward, with an average number of 6.23 persons per dwelling; in 1900 the dwellings numbered 1,282 and the average number of persons in each had increased to 6.34.

The number of voters in the ward is given as follows:

TABLE III
RECORD OF VOTERS

Year	Voters	Year	Voters	Year	Voters
1890	1,358	1900	2,015	1904	2,092
1895	....	1901	2,015	1905	2,093
1898	1,842	1902	1,864	1906	2,028
1899	1,843	1903	1,907	1907	1,843

The number of children in the Second Ward between the ages of five and twenty years increased from 1,970 in 1890 to 2,172 in 1900. Table IV shows the changes in the death rate of this ward since 1890.

TABLE IV

DEATH RATES

Year	Death Rate	Year	Death Rate	Year	Death Rate
1890	14.80	1900	13.80	1904	11.31
1895	17.37	1901	17.20	1905	14.50
1898	12.50	1902	16.40	1906	16.40
1899	12.00	1903	12.17		

There are three schools located within this ward, namely the Webster, Scranton Street and Oak Street schools. The floor and playground space of the first two are given below:

TABLE V

SCHOOL BUILDINGS AND GROUNDS

	Floor Space Sq. Ft.	Playground Space Sq. Ft.
Webster School	18,930	11,000
Scranton Street	27,370	20,000
Oak Street	.....	.....

The figures for contagious diseases are as follows:

TABLE VI

CASES OF CONTAGIOUS DISEASES

Year	Diphtheria	Scarlet Fever	Typhoid	Total	Year	Diphtheria	Scarlet Fever	Typhoid	Total
1890	12	6	7	25	1902	7	37	17	61
1895	6	8	5	19	1903	16	15	8	39
1898	11	2	8	21	1904	13	17	9	39
1899	7	22	10	39	1905	5	22	15	42
1900	4	15	6	25	1906	34	20	30	84
1901	9	6	94	109					

THIRD WARD.

The Third Ward ranks ninth among the wards in area, and in population ranked second both in 1890 and 1900. Its area is approximately 322 acres, of which .06 of an acre only is devoted to park purposes. This ward, too, contains a large cemetery, the Saint Bernard. The population statistics of the ward follow:

TABLE I

POPULATION

Year	Total	White	Colored	Native	Foreign
1890	9,714	9,556	158	5,711	4,003
1900	12,637	12,334	293	7,411	5,226

Here we find the population and its several elements to have increased at the following rates: Total, 30.0 per cent.; Native, 29.7 per cent.; Foreign, 30.5 per cent.; White, 29.0 per cent.; Colored, 85.4 per cent.

These rates of increase are very similar to those for the Second Ward, the only noticeable difference being the even smaller rate for the colored in this ward. The proportions of the colored and foreign born elements to the total population are as follows:

TABLE II

PERCENTAGE OF TOTAL POPULATION

Year	Colored	Foreign
1890	1.6%	41.2%
1900	2.3	41.3

Here we notice a much larger percentage of foreign born than in the first two wards. This is to be explained by the colony of foreign born Jews, mainly Russian, who live in the vicinity of Oak Street and Congress Avenue.

The density of population in this ward was in 1890, 30.1 per acre, and in 1900, 29.2 per acre.

In 1890 there were 1,142 dwellings in the Third Ward, with an average number of 8.51 persons per dwelling; in 1900, the number of dwellings had increased to 1,393, with an average of 9.07 persons per dwellings.

TABLE III

RECORD OF VOTERS

Year	Voters	Year	Voters	Year	Voters
1890	1,813	1900	2,601	1904	2,629
1895	2,082	1901	2,461	1905	2,545
1898	2,239	1902	2,364	1906	2,305
1899	2,287	1903	2,354	1907	2,117

The number of children between five and twenty years of age was 3,196 in 1890, and 4,101 in 1900.

The death rates in this ward since 1890 are given below:

TABLE IV

DEATH RATES

Year	Death Rate	Year	Death Rate	Year	Death Rate
1890	20.7	1900	14.5	1904	13.5
1895	20.0	1901	13.6	1905	13.1
1898	19.5	1902	13.0	1906	15.3
1899	15.0	1903	12.5		

Here we see a very marked decline in the death rate. The rate for the censal year 1900 exhibits a decrease of six deaths per 1,000 population from the rate of 1890. How to account for this decrease I do not know, unless it is because of greater care among the large proportion of foreign born.

There are six schools within the ward, the floor and playground space of which are given in Table V.

TABLE V

SCHOOL BUILDINGS AND GROUNDS

	Floor Space Sq. Ft.	Playground Space Sq. Ft.
Davenport Avenue	4,878	5,076
West Street	5,116	12,000
Cedar Street	26,877	6,000
Hallock Street	8,650	5,000
Welch School	17,616	6,000
Zunder School	22,215	14,000
Total in Ward	85,352	35,076

The figures for the number of cases of contagious diseases appear below:

TABLE VI

CASES OF CONTAGIOUS DISEASES

Year	Diphtheria	Scarlet Fever	Typhoid	Total	Year	Diphtheria	Scarlet Fever	Typhoid	Total
1890	15	9	6	30	1902	11	39	4	54
1895	11	6	4	21	1903	6	7	9	22
1898	16	5	6	27	1904	22	20	15	57
1899	20	19	14	53	1905	20	23	19	62
1900	16	33	6	55	1906	77	19	19	115
1901	24	13	77	114					

FOURTH WARD.

The Fourth Ward ranks seventh among the wards in area and in population ranked first in 1890 as well as in 1900. Its area is 514 acres, of which 24.24 acres are taken up by Bay View Park. A large portion is also taken up by the railroad "Cut" entering New Haven from New York, and as I gather from several persons I have talked with, real estate values in the vicinity of the "Cut," and especially near the roundhouses, have fallen greatly as a result of the "smoke nuisance."

The statistics of the ward's population follow:

TABLE I

POPULATION

Year	Total	White	Colored	Native	Foreign
1890	10,525	10,456	69	7,841	2,684
1900	13,751	13,647	104	9,936	3,815

The percentage increases of the population and its several elements in this ward are found to have been as follows: Total, 30.6 per cent.; Native, 26.7 per cent.; Foreign, 42.1 per cent.; White, 30.5 per cent.; Colored, 50.7 per cent.

The most noticeable thing in the foregoing figures is the large percentile increase of the foreign born in the ward compared with the native increase. This is undoubtedly due in large part to the change in character of occupancy following the fall in real estate values in that section and the increase of soot and noise nuisance to which the native born prove less willing to submit. The proportion of colored and foreign born to the total population of the ward is shown in Table II.

TABLE II

PERCENTAGE OF TOTAL POPULATION

Year	Colored	Foreign Born
1890	0.6%	25.5%
1900	0.7	27.7

By these figures we see that the colored element is very small and that the foreign element occupies about the same proportion to the total population as in the Second Ward.

The density of the population of the Fourth Ward was 20.4 per acre in 1890, and 26.7 per acre in 1900.

In 1890 there were 1,481 dwellings in this ward, with an average number of 7.11 persons per dwelling; the number of dwellings had increased in 1900 to 1,936, with an average number of 7.1 persons per dwelling.

The following table gives the number of voters in the ward:

TABLE III

RECORD OF VOTERS

Year	Voters	Year	Voters	Year	Voters
1890	2,265	1900	3,325	1904	3,358
1895	1,199	1901	3,200	1905	3,342
1898	2,865	1902	3,120	1906	3,160
1899	2,947	1903	3,062	1907	....

The number of children in the Fourth Ward between the ages of five and twenty years increased from 3,057 in the year 1890 to 4,028 in the year 1900.

Table IV exhibits the changes in the death rate of this ward since 1890.

TABLE IV

DEATH RATES

Year	Death Rate	Year	Death Rate	Year	Death Rate
1890	18.2	1900	15.2	1904	14.3
1895	14.9	1901	15.2	1905	16.1
1898	16.4	1902	13.8	1906	17.2
1899	14.3	1903	12.5		

Apparently the rate for this ward is not changing greatly, but whatever change there is seems to point toward a slight decrease.

There are four schools situated within the bounds of the Fourth Ward. The approximate figures for the floor space and playground space of the several schools are given in Table V.

TABLE V

SCHOOL BUILDINGS AND GROUNDS

	Floor Space Sq. Ft.	Playground Space Sq. Ft.
Day School	13,890	5,000
Washington Avenue	13,346	12,743
Greenwich Avenue	4,172	4,000
Kimberly Avenue	12,808	11,000
Total in Ward	44,276	32,743

The figures for contagious diseases appear below:

TABLE VI

CASES OF CONTAGIOUS DISEASES

Year	Diphtheria	Scarlet Fever	Typhoid	Total	Year	Diphtheria	Scarlet Fever	Typhoid	Total
1890	66	11	23	100	1902	16	44	26	86
1895	21	16	10	47	1903	19	38	12	69
1898	29	11	9	49	1904	19	9	14	42
1899	29	20	20	69	1905	16	22	33	71
1900	27	38	11	76	1906	40	21	34	95
1901	13	36	85	134					

FIFTH WARD.

The Fifth Ward stands eleventh in order among the wards in point of area; in population it ranked twelfth both in 1890 and 1900. Its area is 232 acres, of which Waterside Park occupies 18 acres. A large area is taken up by railroad property and freight yards.

TABLE I

POPULATION

Year	Total	White	Colored	Native	Foreign
1890	4,174	4,094	80	2,911	1,263
1900	4,768	4,714	54	2,879	1,889

During this decade the total population of this ward and its several elements changed as follows (a minus sign indicating decrease, otherwise the figures signifying increase): Total, 14.2 per cent.; Native, —1.0 per cent.; Foreign, 49.5 per cent.; White, 15.1 per cent.; Colored, —32.5 per cent.

Apparently this is preeminently the ward of the foreign born, since both the native and colored elements have actually decreased while the foreign element has increased almost 50 per cent. Table II shows the proportion of the colored and foreign elements to the total population of the ward.

TABLE II

PERCENTAGE OF TOTAL POPULATION

Year	Colored	Foreign
1890	1.9%	30.2%
1900	1.1	39.6

The percentage of foreign born is large and is apparently increasing rapidly. It was, in 1900, nearly equal to that of the Third Ward and has probably now surpassed it.

The density of population in the Fifth Ward was 18.00 per acre in 1890, and 20.5 per acre in 1900.

In 1890 there were 559 dwellings in this ward, with an average number of 7.47 persons per dwelling; in 1900, the number of dwellings had decreased to 528 and the average number of persons in each dwelling had risen to 9.03, one of the highest rates attained by any of the wards.

The next table gives the number of voters in the ward.

TABLE III

RECORD OF VOTERS

Year	Voters	Year	Voters	Year	Voters
1890	1,071	1900	1,075	1904	1,117
1895	....	1901	991	1905	1,078
1898	956	1902	1,005	1906	914
1899	949	1903	....	1907	....

The number of children between five and twenty years of age was 1,096 in the year 1890; it increased in 1900 to 1,190.

Table IV shows the changes in the death rate since 1890.

TABLE IV

DEATH RATES

Year	Death Rate	Year	Death Rate	Year	Death Rate
1890	14.9	1901	17.5	1904	21.0
1895	17.7	1902	16.0	1905	21.8
1898	13.9	1903	18.3	1906	24.7
1900	18.6				

Here we see an increase in the death rate of almost four per 1,000 from 1890 to 1900, and an increase of almost ten per 1,000 from 1890 to 1906. This may be due to the large increase of foreign born.

The schools situated within the borders of this ward number three. The figures for the floor space of the individual schools, together with the amount of space available for playground, is given below:

TABLE V

SCHOOL BUILDINGS AND GROUNDS

	Floor Space Sq. Ft.	Playground Space Sq. Ft.
Wooster School	13,336	12,000
Fair Street	14,320	7,800
Whiting Street	1,053	2,000
Total in Ward	28,709	21,800

The figures for the number of cases of the three principal contagious diseases are presented in Table VI.

TABLE VI

CASES OF CONTAGIOUS DISEASES

Year	Diphtheria	Scarlet Fever	Typhoid	Total	Year	Diphtheria	Scarlet Fever	Typhoid	Total
1890	10	2	4	16	1902	3	12	10	25
1895	21	16	10	47	1903	7	9	7	23
1898	9	5	5	19	1904	6	8	19	33
1899	11	3	6	20	1905	4	3	13	20
1900	5	2	7	14	1906	12	2	8	22
1901	9	4	22	35					

APPENDIX.

SIXTH WARD.

The Sixth Ward ranks thirteenth among the wards in area, having but 167 acres, of which 4.66 acres are devoted to park purposes, in Wooster Square. In population it ranked ninth both in 1890 and 1900.

TABLE I
POPULATION

Year	Total	White	Colored	Native	Foreign
1890	5,691	5,647	44	3,453	2,238
1900	6,250	6,227	23	3,676	2,574

The percentile increase of the total population and of its several elements during this decade is as follows, a minus sign indicating a decrease: Total, 9.9 per cent.; Native, 6.5 per cent.; Foreign, 15.0 per cent.; White, 10.2 per cent.; Colored, —0.4 per cent.

The only element in this ward that has increased disproportionately is the foreign born. Their greater increase is undoubtedly due to the fact that the foreign colony of the Fifth Ward is beginning to expand into the Sixth Ward. The following table shows the percentile proportion of colored and foreign elements to the total population of the ward:

TABLE II
PERCENTAGE OF TOTAL POPULATION

Year	Colored	Foreign
1890	0.7%	41.0%
1900	0.3	41.1

Here we see that a large proportion of the population is foreign born, and that the advent of the foreign element apparently drives out the colored.

The density of population in this ward increased from 34 per acre in 1890 to 37.4 per acre in 1900. In the former year there were 629 dwellings, with an average number of 9.05 persons in each; in the latter year the dwellings had increased to 702 and the average number of people in each decreased to 8.9.

The number of voters in this ward for the respective years is as follows:

TABLE III
RECORD OF VOTERS

Year	Voters	Year	Voters	Year	Voters
1890	1,289	1900	1,580	1904	1,550
1895	1,369	1901	1,488	1905	1,482
1898	1,369	1902	1,402	1906	1,353
1899	1,416	1903	1,407	1907	1,287

The number of children between the ages of five and twenty years increased but slightly in the decade—from 1,609 in the year 1890 to 1,710 in the year 1900. Table IV shows the changes in the death rate of this ward since 1890.

TABLE IV
DEATH RATES

Year	Death Rate	Year	Death Rate	Year	Death Rate
1890	22.6	1900	18.4	1904	15.8
1895	16.2	1901	14.4	1905	15.4
1898	17.0	1902	17.4	1906	...
1899	15.0	1903	20.0		

There are two public schools in the Sixth Ward, the Eaton School and the large Hamilton School. The floor space of the Eaton School is approximately 22,431 square feet, and the space available for playground is about 18,000 square feet.

The figures for the number of cases in this ward of the three principal contagious diseases are presented below:

TABLE V
CASES OF CONTAGIOUS DISEASES

Year	Diphtheria	Scarlet Fever	Typhoid	Total	Year	Diphtheria	Scarlet Fever	Typhoid	Total
1890	7	4	4	18	1902	8	16	6	30
1895	4	2	2	8	1903	5	5	10	20
1898	9	1	8	18	1904	4	1	10	15
1899	8	3	7	18	1905	2	3	8	13
1900	1	2	8	11	1906	13	1	16	30
1901	13	7	13	33					

SEVENTH WARD.

The Seventh Ward is the smallest ward in the city in area; in population it ranked third among the wards in 1890, and fourth in 1900. Its area is 154 acres, 3.14 acres of which is taken up by the small park called Jocelyn Square. The figures for the population of the ward are given below:

TABLE I
POPULATION

Year	Total	White	Colored	Native	Foreign
1890	8,594	8,555	39	5,243	3,351
1900	9,504	9,478	26	5,634	3,870

Here we find the population to have increased during the decade as follows, a minus sign indicating a decrease: Total, 10.7 per cent.; Native, 7.4 per cent.; Foreign, 15.4 per cent.; White, 10.7 per cent.; Colored, —33.3 per cent.

The excessive increase of the foreign born accompanying an actual decrease of the colored in the ward is found here as in the Sixth Ward.

The density of population of this ward was 55.8 per acre in 1890, and 61.7 per acre in 1900. This is the greatest density of population for any ward in New Haven.

The number of dwellings increased from 879 in the year 1890 to 977 in the year 1900; the average number of persons per dwelling decreased very slightly—from 9.78 in the former year to 9.72 in the latter. These rates, too, are the highest for any ward in the city and considered together with the density of population, indicate that this section of the city is more congested than any other.

The percentile proportion of colored and foreign population to the total population of the ward is shown in the following table:

TABLE II
PERCENTAGE OF TOTAL POPULATION

Year	Colored	Foreign
1890	0.4%	38.6%
1900	0.2	40.0

A very large proportion again of foreign born, as should be expected from the congestion of the ward, and this foreign element in the ward is growing much faster than the native element.

The number of voters in the ward is given below:

TABLE III
RECORD OF VOTERS

Year	Voters	Year	Voters	Year	Voters
1890	1,839	1900	2,010	1904	2,212
1895	1,958	1901	2,002	1905	2,147
1898	1,922	1902	1,983	1906	2,053
1899	1,900	1903	1,964	1907	2,007

The number of children in the ward between the ages of five and twenty years increased from 2,678 in 1890 to 2,962 in 1900.

Table IV shows the changes in the death rate since 1890.

TABLE IV
DEATH RATES

Year	Death Rate	Year	Death Rate	Year	Death Rate
1890	24.80	1900	19.10	1904	16.7
1895	23.10	1901	19.30	1905	16.6
1898	20.90	1902	15.7	1906	19.0
1899	15.70	1903	21.5		

What changes there have been seem to trend toward a slightly lower death rate. This may perhaps be explained by the supposition that the increase of foreign population came from an influx of middle-aged adults.

There is but one school in the Seventh Ward, the Skinner School. It has a floor space of 13,962 square feet and playground space of about 15,000 square feet.

The figures for the number of cases in this ward of the three principal contagious diseases are presented below:

TABLE V
CASES OF CONTAGIOUS DISEASES

Year	Diphtheria	Scarlet Fever	Typhoid	Total	Year	Diphtheria	Scarlet Fever	Typhoid	Foreign
1890	25	6	2	33	1902	16	27	7	50
1895	10	9	14	33	1903	7	10	11	28
1898	23	7	21	51	1904	8	6	4	18
1899	10	3	8	21	1905	4	9	14	27
1900	6	4	10	20	1906	52	5	29	86
1901	23	19	22	64					

EIGHTH WARD.

The Eighth Ward is eighth in area among the city wards; in population it ranked seventh in 1890 and eighth in 1900. Its area is 485 acres, 43.34 acres of which is in East Rock Park.

TABLE I
POPULATION

Year	Total	White	Colored	Native	Foreign
1890	5,920	5,899	21	4,519	1,401
1900	7,620	7,578	42	5,880	1,740

In this ward the total population and its several elements have increased as follows: Total, 28.7 per cent.; Native, 30.1 per cent.; Foreign, 24.1 per cent.; White, 28.4 per cent.; Colored, 100.0 per cent.

This is the first instance where the foreign born population has increased at a slower rate than the native. Another noticeable feature is the large percentile increase of colored population; but these are so few in actual numbers that their increase does not materially affect the total increase. The foregoing results are just what we should expect in this ward along Whitney Avenue and Orange Street.

The proportion of the colored and foreign born elements to the total population follows:

TABLE II

PERCENTAGE OF TOTAL POPULATION

Year	Colored	Foreign
1890	0.3%	23.8%
1900	0.5	22.8

The density of population in this ward was 12.2 per acre in 1890, and 15.7 per acre in 1900. From 1890 to 1900 the number of dwellings increased from 916 to 1,213; the average number of persons per dwelling decreased from 6.46 to 6.28.

The number of voters in this ward were returned in the years since 1890 as follows:

TABLE III

RECORD OF VOTERS

Year	Voters	Year	Voters	Year	Voters
1890	1,311	1900	1,920	1904	2,036
1895	1,677	1901	1,937	1905	2,041
1898	1,765	1902	1,962	1906	2,087
1899	1,812	1903	1,976	1907	2,123

The number of children between five and twenty years of age in the Eighth Ward increased from 1,655 to 2,013 during the decade 1890 to 1900.

The changes in the death rate since 1890 are shown below:

TABLE IV

DEATH RATES

Year	Death Rate	Year	Death Rate	Year	Death Rate
1890	17.0	1900	14.3	1904	12.6
1895	11.5	1901	10.6	1905	11.3
1898	9.7	1902	11.1	1906	10.5
1899	8.5	1903	12.3		

The general trend of the death rate in the Eighth Ward has been markedly downward. This is to be expected in the more intelligent and highly educated population of that district of the city and it is perfectly logical that this ward should have one of the lowest death rates of any of the wards.

There are four public schools in the ward. Their respective floor space and playground space are given below:

TABLE V

SCHOOL BUILDINGS AND GROUNDS

	Floor Space Sq. Ft.	Playground Space Sq. Ft.
Humphrey Street	5,412	9,000
Lovell School	17,632	11,000
Worthington Hooker School	16,572	3,000
Edwards Street	1,053	4,000
Total in Ward	37,709	21,800

The figures for the number of cases of contagious diseases appear below:

TABLE VI

CASES OF CONTAGIOUS DISEASES

Year	Diphtheria	Scarlet Fever	Typhoid	Total	Year	Diphtheria	Scarlet Fever	Typhoid	Total
1890	29	23	4	56	1902	16	23	11	50
1895	11	16	2	29	1903	..	15	8	23
1898	14	3	6	23	1904	18	7	10	35
1899	3	5	14	22	1905	5	32	10	47
1900	11	1	10	22	1906	21	6	4	31
1901	13	11	18	42					

NINTH WARD.

The Ninth Ward ranks third in area among all the wards of the city, but the first among those wards lying near the center of the city. In population it ranked fourth in 1890 and third in 1900. Its area is 1,034 acres, 17.61 acres of which is in park.

TABLE I

POPULATION

Year	Total	White	Colored	Native	Foreign
1890	8,451	7,084	1,367	6,715	1,736
1900	11,427	9,888	1,539	9,107	2,320

In the Ninth Ward the population and its several elements increased during the decade as follows: Total, 35.2 per cent.; Native, 35.6 per cent.; Foreign, 33.6 per cent.; White, 39.6 per cent.; Colored, 12.5 per cent.

The most noticeable thing in the population statistics of this ward is the comparatively large number of colored, and the fact that the natives are increasing in numbers faster than the foreign and the white faster than the colored. The following table shows the percentile proportion of colored and foreign to the entire population of the ward:

TABLE II

PERCENTAGE OF TOTAL POPULATION

Year	Colored	Foreign
1890	16.1%	20.5%
1900	10.8	20.3

It is certainly noteworthy that the percentage of foreign population in the ward having the largest colored population is comparatively low.

The density of population of this ward was 8.1 per acre in 1890, and 11.0 per acre in 1900.

This does not mean that the population is carefully scattered over the ward with only eleven persons to an acre. As a matter of fact, portions of this ward are pretty well congested, while other portions are not as yet built up at all.

From 1890 to 1900 the number of dwellings in the ward increased in number from 1,377 to 1,828; the average number of persons per dwelling also increased from 6.14 in the former year to 6.26 in the latter.

The number of voters in this ward is given below, as returned in the several years since 1890:

TABLE III

RECORD OF VOTERS

Year	Voters	Year	Voters	Year	Voters
1890	1,811	1900	....	1904	3,124
1895	2,160	1901	2,647	1905	3,028
1898	2,308	1902	2,657	1906	3,027
1899	2,399	1903	2,645	1907	3,059

The number of children between the ages of five and twenty increased from 2,609 to 3,379 during the decade 1890-1900. The changes in the death rate of this ward since 1890 are shown in Table IV.

TABLE IV

DEATH RATES

Year	Death Rate	Year	Death Rate	Year	Death Rate
1890	19.7	1900	15.6	1904	14.2
1895	18.7	1901	16.6	1905	13.0
1898	16.8	1902	15.0	1906	13.9
1899	12.5	1903	11.0		

The death rate in this ward seems to be decreasing steadily. The rate for the censal year 1900 exhibited a decrease of more than four from their rate for 1890.

There are three public schools in the Ninth Ward, also one school maintained in the Saint Francis Orphan Asylum and one in the County Home.

The statistics of the floor and playground space of the three public schools are given below:

TABLE V

SCHOOL BUILDINGS AND GROUNDS

	Floor Space Sq. Ft.	Playground Space Sq. Ft.
Winchester School	17,620	5,000
Shelton Avenue	12,300	6,000
Dixwell Avenue	6,240	10,000
Total in Ward	36,160	21,000

The figures for the number of cases of contagious diseases appear below:

TABLE VI

CASES OF CONTAGIOUS DISEASES

Year	Diphtheria	Scarlet Fever	Typhoid	Total	Year	Diphtheria	Scarlet Fever	Typhoid	Total
1890	56	6	10	72	1902	14	36	29	77
1895	25	28	8	61	1903	21	22	41	84
1898	14	12	7	33	1904	15	22	13	50
1899	17	6	18	41	1905	6	23	16	45
1900	11	38	9	58	1906	18	10	12	40
1901	17	6	90	113					

TENTH WARD.

The Tenth Ward ranks fifth among the wards in area, and in population ranked eighth in 1890 and seventh in 1900. Its area is 602 acres, of which 55.87 acres are taken up by the portion of Edgewood Park within the ward boundaries. The statistics of the ward's population are given in the first table.

TABLE I

POPULATION

Year	Total	White	Colored	Native	Foreign
1890	5,754	5,345	409	4,921	833
1900	7,823	7,349	474	6,736	1,087

From the foregoing figures we find the population and its several elements to have increased during this decade are follows: Total, 36.1 per cent.; Native, 36.8 per cent.; Foreign, 30.4 cent.; White, 37.4 per cent.; Colored, 15.9 per cent.

In this ward, which has rather a large number of colored persons in its population, the colored and foreign born elements are not increasing as fast as the white and native elements. The percentile proportion of the colored and the foreign born to the total population is shown below:

TABLE II

PERCENTAGE OF TOTAL POPULATION

Year	Colored	Foreign
1890	7.1%	14.4%
1900	6.0	13.8

This ward has the smallest percentage of foreign born population of any of the wards in the city proper.

The density of population of the Tenth Ward was 9.25 per acre in 1890, and 12.9 per acre in 1900.

In the former year there were 974 dwellings in the ward, with an average number of 5.91 persons per dwelling; in the latter year the number of dwellings had increased to 1,350 and the average number per dwelling had slightly decreased to 5.79.

The number of voters in the Tenth Ward in the respective years since 1890 is given in Table III.

TABLE III

RECORD OF VOTERS

Year	Voters	Year	Voters	Year	Voters
1890	1,364	1900	1,915	1904	2,070
1895	1,643	1901	1,891	1905	2,054
1898	1,738	1902	1,897	1906	1,954
1899	1,792	1903	1,891	1907	1,983

The number of children between five and twenty years of age in the ward increased from 1,519 to 1,877 during the decade 1890-1900.

The changes in the death rate of this ward since 1890 are to be seen in the following table:

TABLE IV

DEATH RATES

Year	Death Rate	Year	Death Rate	Year	Death Rate
1890	13.2	1900	13.1	1904	12.2
1895	12.7	1901	12.3	1905	16.4
1898	8.2	1902	11.9	1906	13.5
1899	7.5	1903	10.7		

Here we see a death rate somewhat lower than the average for the entire city and that, though fluctuating from year to year, it tends to remain about the same. This is probably due to the more stable character of the population of this section of New Haven.

There are three public schools in this ward, and there is one school in the New Haven Orphan Asylum. The figures for the floor space and the space available for playground of each of the three public schools is given in Table V.

TABLE V

SCHOOL BUILDINGS AND GROUNDS

	Floor Space Sq. Ft.	Playground Space Sq. Ft.
Dwight Street	12,872	5,000
Orchard Street	4,522	6,000
Roger Sherman School	23,916	5,000
Total in Ward	41,310	16,000

The figures for the number of cases of contagious diseases are given below:

TABLE VI

CASES OF CONTAGIOUS DISEASES

Year	Diphtheria	Scarlet Fever	Typhoid	Total	Year	Diphtheria	Scarlet Fever	Typhoid	Total
1890	9	5	4	18	1902	9	17	15	41
1895	1	25	4	30	1903	..	15	33	48
1898	8	6	7	21	1904	11	20	7	38
1899	20	7	14	41	1905	4	11	17	32
1900	5	10	7	22	1906	11	7	23	41
1901	9	4	146	159					

ELEVENTH WARD.

The Eleventh Ward ranks tenth in area among the wards of the city; in population it ranked eleventh in 1890 and tenth in 1900. Its area is 303 acres, 10.84 acres of which is taken up by "Quinnipiac Park." The population statistics of the ward appear below:

TABLE I
POPULATION

Year	Total	White	Colored	Native	Foreign
1890	4,850	4,845	5	3,755	1,095
1900	5,520	5,503	17	4,259	1,261

From the foregoing figures it is found that the ward's total population and its several elements have increased as follows: Total, 13.8 per cent.; Native, 13.4 per cent.; Foreign, 15.1 per cent.; White, 13.5 per cent.; Colored, 240.0 per cent.

The fact to be noticed in this ward is the comparatively even increase of the native and foreign elements. The enormous percentile increase of the colored in the ward is offset by the smallness of their number. The percentile proportion of the colored and foreign born to the total population of the ward is given in Table II.

TABLE II
PERCENTAGE OF TOTAL POPULATION

Year	Colored	Foreign
1890	0.1%	22.5%
1900	0.3	22.8

The density of population in this ward increased from 16.0 per acre in 1890 to 18.2 per acre in 1900. The number of dwellings increased during the same decade from 659 to 839 and the average number of persons per dwelling decreased from 7.36 to 6.57.

The number of voters in this ward, recorded in each of the years in question since 1890, appears below:

TABLE III
RECORD OF VOTERS

Year	Voters	Year	Voters	Year	Voters
1890	1,107	1900	1,394	1904	1,476
1895	1,292	1901	1,396	1905	1,442
1898	1,314	1902	1,409	1906	1,402
1899	1,342	1903	1,394	1907	1,386

The number of children between the ages of five and twenty years was 1,250 in 1890 and 1,579 in 1900.

When we consider that the total population of the ward increased 670 in number, it can readily be seen that the age distribution of this ward must have changed considerably during this decade, since there was an addition of only fifty-nine to the age groups from five to twenty years.

The changes in the death rate of the Eleventh Ward are shown below:

TABLE IV
DEATH RATES

Year	Death Rate	Year	Death Rate	Year	Death Rate
1890	16.6	1900	14.5	1904	12.3
1895	13.4	1901	16.1	1905	12.8
1898	11.9	1902	17.2	1906	13.5
1899	10.3	1903	16.0		

It may be seen from the above figures that the rate in this ward, though fluctuating considerably, has had a slight general trend downwards. Inasmuch as the elements in the ward's population have changed but little in their proportion to one another, this slight general decrease in the death rate may perhaps be explained by an increase in the middle age groups.

There are two public schools in this ward. The figures for their floor space and space available for playing ground are given below:

TABLE V

SCHOOL BUILDINGS AND GROUNDS

	Floor Space Sq. Ft.	Playground Space Sq. Ft.
Woolsey School	15,456	8,000
Lloyd Street	4,562	3,000
Total in Ward.....................	20,018	11,000

The figures for the number of cases of contagious diseases appear below:

TABLE VI

CASES OF CONTAGIOUS DISEASES

Year	Diphtheria	Scarlet Fever	Typhoid	Total	Year	Diphtheria	Scarlet Fever	Typhoid	Total
1890	28	6	28	62	1902	8	9	6	23
1895	4	9	5	18	1903	4	15	2	21
1898	12	2	1	15	1904	8	11	12	31
1899	3	6	2	11	1905	4	10	8	22
1900	10	9	1	20	1906	7	5	12	24
1901	18	12	12	42					

TWELFTH WARD.

The Twelfth Ward ranks fourth in area among the wards of the city; in population it ranked fifth both in 1890 and 1900. The area is 819 acres, 96.21 acres of which is taken up by that portion of East Rock Park contained within the ward boundaries. The ward contains, also, a small cemetery. The statistics of the ward's population are contained in the following table:

TABLE I

POPULATION

Year	Total	White	Colored	Native	Foreign
1890	6,470	6,420	50	4,666	1,804
1900	9,228	9,166	62	6,788	2,440

From the above figures we find the population of this ward and its several elements to have increased at the following rates: Total, 42.6 per cent.; Native, 45.4 per cent.; Foreign, 35.2 per cent.; White, 42.7 per cent.; Colored, 24.0 per cent.

In this ward we find a larger percentile increase in the total population than in any other ward of the city. And the large percentile increase of the native born (again the largest in the city) should also be noted. The proportion of the colored and foreign born elements to the total population of the ward is shown in Table II.

TABLE II

PERCENTAGE OF TOTAL POPULATION

Year	Colored	Foreign
1890	0.7%	27.8%
1900	0.6	26.4

As we should expect from the percentile increases as given above, the proportion of the colored and foreign elements of the total population of the ward slightly decreased during the decade.

The density of population in this ward was 7.8 per acre in 1890, and 11.2 per acre in 1900. From 1890 to 1900 the number of dwellings increased from 944 to 1,366; during the same period the average number of persons per dwelling decreased from 6.85 to 6.75.

The number of voters in this ward, as recorded for the various years in question since 1890, are given below:

TABLE III

RECORD OF VOTERS

Year	Voters	Year	Voters	Year	Voters
1890	1,380	1900	2,219	1904	2,375
1895	1,806	1901	2,197	1905	2,388
1898	1,921	1902	2,221	1906	2,341
1899	2,029	1903	2,235	1907	2,350

The number of children between the ages of five and twenty years was 2,196 in 1890 and 2,776 in 1900.

The very fact of this large increase in the number of persons under twenty years of age would indicate that the increase in the population of this ward was largely native born, even if we had no definite figures showing that such was actually the case, since an increase in the foreign born element would rather tend to increase the population in the older age groups than in those under twenty years.

The changes in the death rate for this ward since 1890 are shown in the following table:

TABLE IV

DEATH RATES

Year	Death Rate	Year	Death Rate	Year	Death Rate
1890	17.9	1900	15.6	1904	15.1
1895	21.8	1901	14.2	1905	14.1
1898	16.5	1902	11.9	1906	14.1
1899	15.1	1903	13.0	1907	...

Except for the one year 1895, the general trend of the rate has been downward, though the decrease has not been so great and apparent as in several other wards.

There are three schools in this ward, the Ezekiel Cheever, Ferry Street and Strong schools. The floor space, and space available for playground of the first two schools, are given in the following table. The estimate for the Strong School was not included among those obtained for me by the Board of Education, so that I am unable to give it. I know, however, that it is one of the largest schools in New Haven and that it has practically no playground space.

TABLE V

SCHOOL BUILDINGS AND GROUNDS

	Floor Space Sq. Ft.	Playground Space Sq. Ft.
Ferry Street	7,204	10,700
Ezekiel Cheever School	10,662	6,500
Strong School	.....	....

The figures for the number of cases that have occurred in the ward of the three principal contagious diseases appear below:

TABLE VI

CASES OF CONTAGIOUS DISEASES

Year	Diphtheria	Scarlet Fever	Typhoid	Total	Year	Diphtheria	Scarlet Fever	Typhoid	Tota
1890	30	8	11	49	1902	9	21	8	38
1895	6	8	17	31	1903	16	28	8	52
1898	14	4	10	28	1904	7	21	18	46
1899	15	4	14	33	1905	16	18	16	50
1900	16	11	8	35	1906	24	10	22	56
1901	22	42	18	82					

THIRTEENTH, FOURTEENTH AND FIFTEENTH WARDS.

Before starting on the statistics of the Thirteenth, Fourteenth and Fifteenth wards, it will be well to preface them with a few remarks. In the first place, these are the "new" wards of the city, the last two having been legally a part of the city only since 1897. The census for 1890, however, gives the total population of each of these wards, but does not give the figures for the several elements of the population, nor does it give any other information concerning the wards. Hence, for this other information we have only the census figures for 1900, and there can of course be no comparison with the earlier census year. Westville, the Thirteenth Ward, has a separate school system and I have at hand no information in regard to it. Previous to 1897 there are no separate death rates computed for the Fourteenth and Fifteenth wards, as they were still grouped together in "Fair Haven East." To save space the three wards are grouped together in the following tables.

The Thirteenth Ward ranks first in area among the city wards; in population it ranked thirteenth both in 1890 and 1900. The Fourteenth and Fifteenth wards combined rank second in area; in population they ranked respectively fourteenth and fifteenth in 1890, and fifteenth and fourteenth in 1900.

Their area and population are given below in the first table:

TABLE I

POPULATION AND AREA

	Population		Area in Acres
	1890	1900	
Thirteenth Ward	1,975	2,695	3,058
Fourteenth Ward	1,696	1,851 }	3,047
Fifteenth Ward	1,076	1,969 }	

Of the total area of the Thirteenth Ward, 252.68 acres are in West Rock Park, and of the Fifteenth Ward, 66.02 acres are in Fort Hale and Fort Wooster parks.

The density of population of these wards was as follows: Thirteenth Ward—0.6 per acre in 1890, and 0.8 per acre in 1900; Fourteenth and Fifteenth wards—0.9 per acre in 1890, and 1.2 per acre in 1900.

These three wards are naturally the most sparsely settled regions of the city. The last two wards are increasing in density of population slightly faster than the Thirteenth Ward.

From the figures of Table I we find the population of these three wards to have increased during the period from 1890 to 1900 at the following rates: Thirteenth Ward, 36.4 per cent.; Fourteenth Ward, 9.1 per cent.; Fifteenth Ward, 83.0 per cent.

The rate of increase for the Fifteenth Ward, if a true one, is really remarkable; but the United States Census Commission may have divided the two wards differently in 1900 and 1890. The very low rate of increase for the Fourteenth Ward would seem to substantiate this belief.

The proportion of the colored and foreign born to the total population in each of the three wards in 1900 is given in the following table:

TABLE II

POPULATION IN 1900

	Total Population	Total Colored	Total Foreign	Per cent. Colored	Per cent. Foreign
Thirteenth Ward	2,695	30	811	1.1%	30.1%
Fourteenth Ward	1,851	11	289	0.6	15.6
Fifteenth Ward	1,969	..	453	...	23.0

The only noteworthy thing here is the total absence of any colored element in the Fifteenth Ward.

The number of dwellings and the average number of persons per dwelling in each of the three wards in 1900 was as follows: Thirteenth Ward, 479 dwellings, 5.62 persons per dwelling; Fourteenth Ward, 378 dwellings, 4.89 persons per dwelling; Fifteenth Ward, 391 dwellings, 5.35 persons per dwelling.

The number of voters recorded in each of these wards in the various years in question is shown by Table III.

TABLE III

RECORD OF VOTERS

Year	Thirteenth Ward	Fourteenth Ward	Fifteenth Ward	Year	Thirteenth Word	Fourteenth Ward	Fifteenth Ward
1890	468	424	270	1902	571	476	500
1895	558	454	352	1903	574	464	496
1898	612	474	390	1904	632	496	521
1899	627	486	418	1905	637	497	518
1900	690	483	512	1906	649	517	525
1901	712	478	491	1907	700	503	558

The number of children between the ages of five and twenty years was in 1900, in the Thirteenth Ward, 685, in the Fourteenth Ward, 512, and in the Fifteenth Ward, 588.

The changes in the death rate of these wards is shown in Table IV.

TABLE IV

DEATH RATES

Year	Thirteenth Ward	Fourteenth Ward	Fifteenth Ward	Year	Thirteenth Ward	Fourteenth Ward	Fifteenth Ward
1890	19.4	...	...	1902	12.0	15.6	12.5
1895	11.8	...	...	1903	9.5	14.3	14.5
1898	14.4	15.2	11.3	1904	10.6	18.7	11.1
1899	10.4	10.0	16.6	1905	16.3	10.6	14.5
1900	12.6	14.5	13.3	1906	14.9	17.0	13.1
1901	11.1	14.5	13.3				

There are two public schools in the Fourteenth Ward and two in the Fifteenth Ward. The statistics of their floor space and playground space are given below:

TABLE V

SCHOOL BUILDINGS AND GROUNDS

	Floor Space Sq. Ft.	Playground Space Sq. Ft.
Lenox Street	3,084	7,000
Quinnipiac Avenue	6,150	15,000
Total in Fourteenth Ward	9,234	22,000

	Floor Space Sq. Ft.	Playground Space Sq. Ft.
Woodward School	13,580	12,000
Morris Cove School	1,118	17,000
Total in Fifteenth Ward	14,698	29,000

SUMMARY.

Having surveyed the city entire and the city as divided into its fifteen wards, let us attempt to sum up the more important facts that we have at hand, tending to show the nature and direction of the city's growth. Referring first to the figures showing the percentile increase of the total population (and its several elements) in each ward, we deduce the following results.

Aside from the Fifteenth Ward, which seems to be increasing in population at such a rapid rate that it almost doubled during the decade 1890-1900, the wards which are developing most rapidly are the Twelfth, Tenth and Ninth, with rates respectively of 42.6, 36.1, and 35.2 per cent. This shows that the development of New Haven is following two directions, one toward Westville and Highwood, the other out along the western bank of the Quinnipiac River past Cedar Hill toward East Rock. The direction of growth out toward Westville is emphasized by growth of Westville itself, which increased 36.4 per cent. from 1890 to 1900. The Second, Third and Fourth wards have the next largest percentile increases, 30.6, 30.0 and 30.6 per cent., respectively. The Second Ward adjoins the Tenth Ward, and again emphasizes the trend of the city's growth toward Westville. The large increases in the Third and Fourth wards are probably due to the fact that these wards have received a large influx of foreign born; as this element in the Fourth Ward increased 42.1 per cent. during the decade. The Eighth Ward ranks next in rapidity of growth. The considerable increase of this ward also emphasizes the growth out toward the eastern base of East Rock.

Considering the population by its several elements, we find the white population increasing fastest in the wards having the greatest total increase in population. The colored element, on account of its paucity of numbers, has a great irregularity of increase. It is noteworthy that in the Ninth and Tenth wards, where the colored element bears a larger proportion to the total population than in any other of the wards, it is increasing more slowly than the white element. The only wards in the city proper in which the relative increase of the native born during the decade was greater than that of the foreign born, are the Eighth, Ninth, Tenth and Twelfth. The Fifth Ward, with its actual decrease of 1 per cent. among the native born and its increase of 49.5 per cent. among the foreign born, seems destined to become the most thoroughly foreign part of the city. True, the percentage of foreign born in that ward was not quite so large in 1900 as that in the Third, Sixth and Seventh wards, but the rate of increase was greater, and probably by now the percentage of foreign born to total population is the largest in the city. In the Fourth Ward the foreign born increased also at a very rapid rate from 1890 to 1900. Next to the Fifth Ward the Third Ward is the most distinctively foreign quarter of New Haven; it showed an increase of 30.5 per cent. in the decade in question, and a foreign population in 1900 that was 41.3 per cent.

Looking at just the per cent. of foreign born in the various wards in 1890 and 1900, we discover the following facts. In 1890, the Third, Sixth, Seventh and Fifth wards had the largest per cents of foreign born, in the order named, with the first three each having about 40 per cent., and the last having only 30.2 per cent; in 1900, however, although the order remains the same, the first two had about 41 per cent., the third 40 per cent., and the last-named had crept up to 39.6 per cent.

The only wards with any considerable proportion of colored population are the Ninth and Tenth, with percentile proportions of 16.1 and 7.1, respectively, in 1890; and 10.8 and 6.0 in 1900.

The Seventh Ward is far and away the most thickly populated of the wards, with its density of 55.8 per acre in 1890 and 61.7 in 1900. The Sixth Ward ranked next, with a density of 34.0 per acre in 1890, but in 1900 it was passed by the Third Ward, which increased in density during the decade from 30.1 to 39.2, while the Sixth Ward followed close with a density of 37.4. The wards that were the most thinly populated in 1890 increased most rapidly during the decade, namely, the Ninth, Tenth, Twelfth and Thirteenth. Of the wards in the center of the city, the Second Ward had the smallest density of population both in 1890 and 1900.

Considering the statistics for the average number of persons dwelling in the various wards, again we find the Seventh Ward leading, with an average of 9.78 persons per dwelling in 1890, and 9.72 in 1900. The Sixth Ward with 9.05 had the next highest average in 1890, but in 1900 it was passed by the Third and Fifth wards. This would seem to indicate that building activity in the Sixth Ward is more than keeping pace with the growing of the population; while the large increase in the number of persons per dwelling in the Third and Fifth wards apparently means that the increase of the population of these two wards (which was rather large during the decade) has not been met by a corresponding increase in the number of buildings. The only other ward besides the Sixth, in which the average number of persons per dwelling has decreased to any appreciable extent, is the Eleventh. It is noteworthy here that the Eleventh Ward adjoins the Sixth and is practically an extension of the Sixth out to the Quinnipiac River. This fact probably may be taken to mean that these wards are the only section of the city wherein the number of buildings is increasing proportionately faster than the population.

I will conclude this summary with a glance at the death rates of the various wards in the censal years 1890 and 1900. These rates are all contained in the table below. But first, let it be understood that no death rate is an absolute index of the healthfulness of a community. So many factors enter into the death rate that it is impossible to compare the crude rates of any two communities unless those two communities are under identically the same conditions of age distribution and made up of the same proportions of the same race elements. Of course the different wards of the city are *not* made up of the same race elements nor, as has been pointed out in several specific wards, is the age distribution of population the same in all the wards. Consequently no *absolute* deductions can be made from the following table:

TABLE I

DEATH RATES

	1890	1900		1890	1900
First Ward	12.1	11.0	Ninth Ward	19.7	15.6
Second Ward	14.8	13.8	Tenth Ward	13.2	13.1
Third Ward	20.7	14.5	Eleventh Ward	16.6	14.5
Fourth Ward	18.2	15.2	Twelfth Ward	17.9	15.6
Fifth Ward	14.9	18.6	Thirteenth Ward	19.4	12.6
Sixth Ward	22.6	18.4	Fourteenth Ward	...	14.5
Seventh Ward	24.8	19.1	Fifteenth Ward	...	13.3
Eighth Ward	17.0	14.3			

The Fifth Ward is the only ward in the city in which the death rate increased during the decade. The increase, it seems to me, is explained by the very large increase in the foreign born population, the largest percentile increase in any ward in the city. It should also be noted that the Seventh Ward, which has the greatest density of population, the largest average number of persons per dwelling and one of the largest percentages of foreign born, had the highest death rate in 1890 and again in 1900. The Sixth Ward, which ranked second in both years in proportion of foreign to total population and which had the second greatest density of population in the earlier year, had the second highest death rate in 1890 and third highest in 1900. The lowest death rate in each of the years in question, as might be expected from the make-up of the ward, is found in the First Ward; the next lowest is in the Second Ward.

In making this statistical investigation into the social and economic tendencies of the city, the chief difficulties were found in the inadequacy of the records kept by the city, and in the biased errors of the records which so often arise from the fact that each department of the administration generally compiles its own statistics and naturally attempts to make the figures read as favorably as possible to itself. The former difficulty cannot be avoided; the latter I have attempted to eliminate by correction in some cases and in others by comparison of the different results of several authorities, wherever such exist. Nearly every department of the city administration of New Haven has been laid under contribution and they have all been very kind in lending every assistance within their power.

Ronald M. Byrnes.

APPENDIX—PART II.

BUILDING LINES IN THE FIRST WARD OF NEW HAVEN.

REPORT OF FREDERICK LAW OLMSTED

TO THE JOINT COMMITTEE OF THE CIVIC FEDERATION AND THE CHAMBER OF COMMERCE
ON STREETS AND BUILDING LINES.

Mr. William S. Pardee,

Quinnipiack Club, New Haven, Conn.

Dear Sir:—You have asked me to express an opinion in regard, to building lines for the streets of the First Ward now under consideration. Having renewed my acquaintance with the streets in question by an examination thereof on the ground in company with your Committee and with the aid of a set of prints from the City Engineer's office, showing the buildings, the street lines and certain building lines as defined in various past ordinances, I beg to report as follows:

In order to decide wisely upon any specific building line problem it is almost essential to divide the question into two parts and to answer those parts separately. The first part is: "At what final result can the City wisely aim in dealing with the street in question?" The second is: "What steps are most expedient for attaining that result and when can they most expediently be taken?"

The purpose in view in establishing a building line is apt to be twofold: on the one hand the maintenance of adequate space for light and air and for agreeable appearance; on the other hand the avoidance of new buildings within a zone which may be needed at some future time for a widening of the street to accommodate increased traffic. Sometimes one of these purposes is dominant and sometimes the other, and it is important to analyze the probable future uses of any given street rather carefully in order to see what kind of a building line, if any, is ultimately desirable.

For example, where the main purpose of establishing a building line is to maintain proper space for light and air, etc., and where provision for increased traffic space is needless, there is no objection to considerable variation in the width between building lines; in fact, the most logical arrangement with such local or non-thoroughfare streets is to allow a smaller distance between buildings at the points where they enter main streets and to require a wider setback throughout the rest of the blocks. The corner houses get plenty of light and air from the wider streets in any case and the valuable frontage of the main streets is by this plan not needlessly curtailed. So far as appearance is concerned, providing that the architecture of the projecting buildings is at all respectable and takes any sort of advantage of the situation, the appearance of a local or non-thoroughfare street which thus widens out after one enters it is apt to be very pleasing, especially on residence streets. This practice is commonly and intelligently applied in many of the cities of Northern Europe and it is interesting to note that it was followed, though somewhat timidly, in the ordinances of the '70s which defined building lines for the non-thoroughfare streets of the First Ward of New Haven,—Wall, High, Crown and George streets.

When I refer to the building line ultimately desirable it implies a very long look ahead. There is every reason to believe that most of the existing streets of New Haven will be located just where they now are, with comparatively minor changes, not only until after all the present buildings shall have disappeared and shall have been replaced by others, but after that process has been repeated scores of times with the lapse of passing centuries. The future of the City is so long a period that if the burden can be properly distributed no conceivable improvement which would really increase the efficiency of the street system can be regarded as forever impossible. This does not mean that it would be wise or even possible for the present generation to assume the burden of ensuring, by the establishment of building lines, all of the street widenings the ultimate value of which can be clearly foreseen; but it does mean that it is the duty of this generation first to fix its aim a long way ahead and then to make up its mind just how far it can reasonably afford to go in pursuit of that aim.

Considering first the future needs of general street traffic passing through the First Ward, it is obvious that Chapel and Elm streets must always be the principal east and west thoroughfares. The convergence of Elm and Goffe streets with Whalley and Dixwell avenues from the west and northwest, and of Grand Avenue, St. John Street and State Street from the east and northeast, will in time throw a very heavy traffic on Elm Street through the First Ward. It is needless to explain the importance of Chapel Street as a thoroughfare. Grove Street and George Street are thoroughfares only secondary to Elm and Chapel streets, while Crown and Wall streets are not thoroughfares at all, and are unlikely ever to receive a considerable traffic.

Of the north and south streets the thoroughfares of great permanent importance are State and Church streets. Temple Street also is important as a relief line for Church Street. York Street is a secondary thoroughfare of some importance like Grove Street. College Street is a thoroughfare of very secondary importance, since Prospect Street, of which it is the outlet, is limited by hills on the north, and College Street itself has no good outlet to the south. Orange Street is in much the same class as College Street except that it may become valuable as a line of relief for State and Church streets, passing as it does through the center of the narrow neck of business territory between the railroad and the Green.

From the point of view of future traffic requirements Elm, Chapel, State, and Church streets may be regarded as thoroughfares of first class importance, and Grove, George, York, and Temple streets as important secondary thoroughfares, with Orange and College streets in a special category following them.

For a thoroughfare of the first class, carrying two car tracks and lined on both sides by buildings in front of which it is necessary for vehicles to stop, the least width between curbs that will permit an ordinary wagon to pass between a car and a wagon standing at the curb is about 50 feet, and as much as 54 or 55 feet is very desirable to give good clearance. Adding proper sidewalks, we have 80 feet as a close minimum width for such thoroughfares and 90 or 100 feet as desirable. When it is considered that the average depth of the blocks fronting on the main thoroughfares of the First Ward is over 370 feet and the least depth 330 feet, it seems to me not unreasonable to look forward to the time, within a hundred years or so, when the almost useless backyards of these deep lots will be curtailed by enough to give adequate width to the streets.* In view of the expectation indicated above it would seem desirable, in establishing any building lines on the four main thoroughfares, to consider a sufficient setback to keep open the way for a future widening of the streets to at *least* 80 feet. I will therefore take up those four streets in order:

Elm Street appears to be 66 feet wide, except opposite the Green, where it is more. East of Temple Street a building line is shown as of August 8, 1872, calling for a setback of 4 feet

* See table of depths of lots on last page.

on each side except at certain corners, where it is 2 feet. Most of the buildings are set back considerably further than this old building line not only where the line was drawn but also west of Temple Street. The exceptions on the north side are as follows: 1, a brick block on the corner of State and Elm streets which protrudes beyond the line of Grand Avenue produced and will cause in time a very bad obstruction to east and west traffic; 2, a brick block on the corner of Orange Street; 3, the new brick building of the Security Insurance Co. on the corner of Church Street; 4, a couple of small store buildings on the corner of York Street. If one wood and two brick dwellings near Church Street be included, I believe there are no other buildings within twelve or fourteen feet north of the present street line, and all the lots are deep. On the south side about an equal number of buildings project beyond the old building line, of which the most prominent is the Presbyterian Church; but most of the other buildings do not stand back as far as those on the north side and there are some shallow lots. It would seem desirable to aim at preventing the erection of any additional buildings within about twelve or fourteen feet back of the street line on the north side and within about four feet on the south side; and in addition whenever a new building comes to be erected upon the northwest corner of Elm and State streets that corner should be clipped on a diagonal so as to give direct entrance to Elm Street from Grand Avenue. The question of how far to proceed at the present time in view of the above conclusions will be discussed in general terms below.

Chapel Street appears to vary from $63\frac{1}{2}$ to about 66 feet, except opposite the Green, where it widens toward the north. East of Temple Street an old building line is indicated calling for a 3 or 4 foot setback, but practically all the buildings appear to be on the street line. West of Temple Street no building line is indicated but many of the buildings are set back. On the north side of Chapel from College to York streets a large proportion of the property belongs to Yale University and the University Buildings appear to be set back about 20 feet or more. It would seem clearly desirable to maintain this setback throughout the three blocks in question, thus securing at a comparatively small effort a clear width of some 86 feet along Chapel Street from Church to the west boundary of the ward. East of Church Street the establishment of any building lines with a view to a future effective widening must be a costly matter, but looking to the remoter future it cannot be denied that such a widening will in time become very desirable. Moreover in view of the distance of 360 feet or more between Chapel and Court streets such a widening would not curtail the size of the lots undesirably. The difficulty is one of how and when to bring about such a change without making the burden of accomplishing the necessary adjustments too severe or inequitable. Fortunately there appears to be less need for taking immediate action here than at other points in the ward where conditions are changing more rapidly.

As to State Street and as to Church Street from Chapel to George almost the same might be said as about Chapel Street east of Church. On State Street conditions are less definitely established, values are lower, and a few buildings still stand back of the street line. The width of the street has been encroached upon, reducing it at places to considerably less than the theoretical 66 feet, while as a thoroughfare it is by location the natural channel of one of the greatest if not the very greatest stream of general traffic in the City. On account of the railroad location to the east, if any widening of State Street is ever to be made it can probably best be made on the west side, and a building line is ultimately to be desired on that side. On Church Street south of Chapel the old building lines, three feet back of the street lines, have been pretty generally observed on the east side and on that side ought now to be confirmed. On the west side the conditions are very much the same as on Chapel and State streets and there appears to remain only a hope that something may be accomplished at some indefinite future time. Church Street north of the Green is scarcely over 62 feet wide. The old building lines are 8 feet back from the street on each side. On the east side of the street the building of the Security Insurance Co. on the corner of Elm Street appears to stand on the street line, five wooden dwellings appear to stand about 4 feet back and the remainder of the buildings appear to stand back of the old building lines. On the west side all the buildings appear to stand from 15 to 27 feet back of the street line, except for one bay window. The jog in alignment with Whitney Avenue at the north end of Church Street and with the wider part of the street at the Green, as well as the present disposition of buildings, suggests the desirability of a greater ultimate widening on the west than on the east side. It would seem wise therefore to look forward to the prevention of additional buildings within the old building line on the east and within a line about 15 feet back on the west side so as to provide for an ultimate clear width of more than 80 feet. The question of an additional setback on the corner of Grove Street to allow for a good junction with the angular direction of Whitney Avenue is to be seriously considered.

Grove Street appears to be sixty feet wide and the old building lines were set ten feet back on each side so as to secure a clear width of 80 feet throughout. This seems a desirable aim and nothing in the present situation suggests that it would be better to divide the additional space unequally between the two sides. As to York Street, I have no copy of that section of the map at hand at the time of writing this report, but my recollection is that most of the buildings now stand back from the street on the east side and that there is an old building line on that side. It would be desirable here also to secure 80 feet between buildings. On George Street no old building line appears to have been drawn and I have not studied the matter sufficiently to express an opinion as to whether it is worth while to aim at an ultimate widening, but as the street is only about 53 feet wide and is in a position to afford a valuable line of relief for Chapel Street, the presumption is in favor of its ultimate widening. It is a matter, however, which needs to be studied as regards the whole street as a thoroughfare and not with regard merely to the portion in the First Ward. College Street is about 64 feet wide and the old building lines provided an 8 foot setback on each side so as to secure ultimately an 80 foot clear width. In view of the necessary use of this street by the carline from the district between Prospect Hill and the tracks of the Northampton Division, I am inclined to think the old lines, especially to the north of Chapel Street, were wisely chosen.

Orange Street, south of Elm, is only 42 to 44 feet wide, is at most points closely lined with buildings and a considerable number of the lots are rather shallow. It is not likely to have car tracks forced upon it. No old building line appears to have been defined for this portion. On the whole it seems doubtful whether it would prove worth while to attempt a general widening of this street for traffic purposes. North of Elm Street, Orange Street appears to be from $44\frac{1}{2}$ to $52\frac{1}{2}$ feet wide; except for five lots with a total frontage of 80 feet which are from 100 to 102 feet deep and one corner lot of an average depth of about 75 feet, the lots range from 115 to 150 feet deep. The old building lines called for a setback of 10 feet except for corner lots, where only a 4 foot setback was required for a length of 60 feet. This is an example of a building line established not with a view to a future widening for traffic purposes but for the sake of preserving adequate light and air and an orderly and spacious appearance. I believe that the principle upon which these old lines were based was a sound one and appropriate to such a street as Orange Street. With some modification, perhaps, of the precise length and amount of the corner lot offsets of the old building lines, it would be desirable to reestablish them, although not a matter so vital to the City at large as the main thoroughfare building lines previously discussed. On Temple Street the only old building line indicated on my notes is one of a 10 foot setback on the west side south of Chapel. There are none north of Elm. The best opportunity for widening Temple Street as a relief for Church and in connection with any direct avenue of approach to the Railroad Station appears to be upon the east side, and it is upon that side, if upon either, that a building line should be applied; but this is a case of so radical a change, and one in which the cost of imposing a building line would run to so large a proportion of the cost of actually widening the street, that no building line seems to be called for here without much further consideration.

The remaining streets of the Ward are not thoroughfares and are likely always to remain local streets. Those upon which old building lines are indicated are Crown, High, Court and Wall streets. East of Temple, Crown Street is about 45 feet wide and the old building lines are 2 feet back except near the corners, where they are one foot back. On the north side about three-fifths of the frontage appears to be occupied by buildings on the street line, the remainder being from a foot and a half to some 6 feet back. On the south side all the buildings, except one at the corner of State Street, appear to be back of the building line, some of them several feet back. It would seem reasonable to make the building line conform with the street line on the north side and to set it back slightly on the south, at least as far as the old line, possibly farther. The street line is far from straight, and a new building line would naturally not be exactly parallel with it. West of Temple Street the old building lines are 10 feet back and about half of the buildings are back of them. Most of the remainder are 5 feet back. With a few exceptions, mostly where rear buildings have been introduced to utilize the excessive depth, the lots are deep, and still contain a good deal of vacant land. It would seem not unreasonable to re-establish the old building lines, perhaps with exceptions on the corners, in accordance with the principle previously discussed. Court Street is about 40 feet wide and the old building lines were 4 feet back. Between Orange and Church streets most of the buildings are on the street line, one of them over the line. East of Orange Street about half the buildings are about on the old building line and the rest on or near the street line. A considerable proportion of the lots are shallow. It is very doubtful whether any building setback on this street is worth while. Wall Street and High Street are both cases where a fairly liberal building line with reduced setback at the corners, on the principle employed in the old building lines for these streets, would be desirable, the precise amount of the setback depending somewhat on the attitude of the abutters.

If it is felt that the City cannot afford to incur at this time the expense of establishing all the building lines that will ultimately be needed to safeguard the space along all the streets where building is likely to occur in the near future, I would call your attention to another possible method of procedure. Since the line upon any given street or block may be made to vary in the amount of setback required, it can be so adjusted for the time being in special cases as to avoid properties where the desirable building line would give rise to damages largely in excess of the benefits. But instructions could nevertheless be given to the Building Department to notify the proper authorities upon receipt of an application for a permit to build upon any of the properties so avoided, and action could be taken at that time for altering the building line to include such portion of the property in question as might be necessary to conform to the ultimately desirable plan. The advantage of this method is simply that it postpones action by the City in respect to the properties in question, and therefore postpones the incurring of any liability for damages, until the last possible moment before the right of preventing the erection of a new building on the land in question must be exercised. This postponement means a saving in interest charges to the City, probably sufficient to cover the increased damages due to rising land values, and it would distribute the burden on the generations that reap the benefit instead of piling it up on the generation that has the foresight to arrange the machinery for accomplishing the future good.

This method of preparing a thoroughgoing, bold and comprehensive plan of building lines and future street improvements, and then acting on it only block by block or lot by lot at such times as the owners get ready to build or rebuild, is employed a good deal in European cities and is under many circumstances a sensible and economical procedure. In this country, in case we cannot afford to establish a plan and put it into effect once for all, we are apt to give it up as hopeless. Of course it is simple and more satisfactory to establish the ideal permanent building lines for a whole street or a whole ward or a whole city at one operation and have it over with; but if we cannot afford the luxury of such a wholesale procedure, is it not worth while to decide on what is wanted and peg away at it patiently even if in places it has to be done by one or two lots at a time? A serious difficulty in following out such a gradual systematic policy in the average American city is that the City Council changes too rapidly to enable it to supply the needed continuity of initiative. Such work needs to be done by relatively permanent administrative officers acting under the control of the Council as to rate of expenditure and general policy. A permanent Building Line Commission constituted somewhat after the manner of a Park Commission and acting through a Building Line Bureau in the City Engineer's Department, might be well adapted to accomplish the purposes in view. They would from time to time cause plans to be prepared for proposed building lines, and would submit the same from time to time to the City Council. The Council would make contingent appropriations from time to time, to be available for meeting the cost of legally establishing such parts of the approved proposed lines as the activity of building operations in various districts might render expedient. A reasonable annual appropriation to this contingent fund would allow the establishment of building lines to keep in advance of the operation of building out to the street lines of narrow streets and would finally result in getting such lines established wherever they are needed, without throwing excessive burdens upon any one administration or allowing important streets to be throttled because of the lack of any means of securing prompt action by the City. Probably the best sort of body for dealing with this building line question would be one constituted after the manner of the Hartford City Plan Commission and with similar broad duties in addition to those of determining building lines.

Respectfully submitted,

FREDERICK LAW OLMSTED.

Note:—The following table indicates the depths of the present lots fronting on the four main thoroughfares of the First Ward as accurately as obtainable from the maps at hand:

DEPTH OF LOTS	PERCENTAGE OF TOTAL FRONTAGE OCCUPIED BY LOTS OF THE VARIOUS DEPTHS INDICATED			
	State Street	Elm Street	Church Street	Chapel Street
40′ – 60′	2%	....	....	..′.
60 – 80	13	3%	5%	16%
80 –100	9	4	2	5
100 –120	15	13	21	12
120 –150	14	13	14	21
150′ and over	34	62	41	44
Sides of corner lots fronting on other streets..	13	5	17	2
	100%	100%	100%	100%

THE FATE OF THE 1910 PLAN

by Douglas W. Rae

The 1910 Plan justly celebrated here is an intelligent and grounded exercise in City Beautiful planning. Yet only a handful of its ninety-three proposals reached New Haven pay dirt. Most were picked off by the politics of an industrial city whose mayor aspired to such things as uniform cement sidewalks and high Republican turnout. At a deeper level, it ran into an urbanism where the vast majority of heavy lifting was performed outside government. If industrial growth drove up the grand list, boosted the supply of paid work, and attracted eager newcomers from across the globe, a relatively passive city could look pretty strong.

The impetus to found New Haven's Civic Improvement Committee, hence to commission the Gilbert and Olmsted report, came from Yale instructor George Dudley Seymour. In 1907, his 11,000-word public letter sought to elevate public purpose above self-interest, civics above commerce. Citing City Beautiful projects from Buffalo to Cleveland, Paris, London, and Washington D.C., Seymour pressed hard for a unified, top-down planning vision: "The laying out of every street and the placing of every public building should proceed on a definite and controlling idea, there should be a dominant principle of design, an adaptation to an end clearly seen, an effort to weld all together into one balanced composition. To these requirements should be added courage—a certain audacity."[1]

In the founding era of New Haven Colony (ca. 1637) a similarly unified vision had been dominant within the little theocracy. Its mark is still visible in the three-by-three grid of the major colonial streets. This vision had since been sliced to pieces by generations of fresh streets and buildings. In 1907, Gilbert and Olmsted thus confronted the inconvenience of streets already laid out and public buildings long since placed.

Growth, hustle, ingenuity: these were the slogans of New Haven in the early twentieth century. Sixty years earlier, in 1850, New Haven had been a marginal port city of 20,345. By 1910, it had become a dynamic industrial city of 133,605. Winchester Repeating Arms, Sargent Hardware, Candee Rubber, and New Haven Clock employed tens of thousands. A score of other firms produced other goods, from ladders and small boats to canned meat and religious arts. Immigrants from southern and eastern Europe came as fast as new jobs presented themselves. New Haven saw itself as a strategically blessed place in which to manufacture hardware, guns, rubber goods, industrial machinery, clocks, and watches:

The right place to manufacture successfully is evidently at a point where materials accumulate naturally, is contiguous to and has easy access from the original sources of supply, and where, at the same time, there is cheap power, cheap fuel, and advanced and ample facilities for marketing the products. New Haven has always furnished these conditions in preeminent degree. Situated at a focal point of six railroads, connecting the city with markets of the East and West, the lumber regions of the North, and the coal fields of the South, and bordered by the water of the Sound, with a harbor and channel that accommodate ships of the largest size, material necessarily accumulates here, and cheap power is amply provided and assured for all time.[2]

Subsequent developments suggest that this last boast can be counted as true only if "cheap power . . . assured for all time" is qualified by "assured until the 1940s." Today, greater New Haven has energy costs in the top 1 percent of such costs nationwide.[3]

The 1910 report itself had been financed with gifts of $100 (Roughly $2,300 today) from the industrial and professional leadership of New Haven. None could have been expected to finance any major part of *administration and construction* for all the buildings, streets, parks, and playgrounds contemplated by Gilbert and Olmsted. Who then might pay and oversee all this?

The report was submitted to Mayor Frank Rice in December of 1910. Rice had been mayor less than a year, after advocating uniform sidewalks as a key part of his inaugural. His modest year-end statement was the soul of parsimony: "We have worked to the best end with the limited money at hand. The appropriations have been none too large and our endeavor has been to make the best showing with the money in hand. . . . I should say that, in my opinion, the best work has been done in improving the city sidewalks."[4] Rice was being modest and parsimonious; he wasn't being altogether transparent. The aldermen had created a seven-member city plan commission in response to the report. George Dudley Seymour—initiator of the whole enterprise, then secretary of the city plan commission—would write three decades later: "Mayor Rice was not in favor of city planning, notwithstanding the fact that cities and towns, not just in the United States but throughout the world, were engaging in turning to its advantages. . . . In his annual budgets, Mayor Rice never asked for any appropriation for the work of the commission. . . . Mayor Rice would not allow the Secretary [Seymour] to call meetings of the commission, nor would he fix upon a plan of scheduled meetings."[5]

Within the next year, Seymour would resign as secretary. Rice may well have resented outside experts bent on supplanting "local prejudice." He may have resented a report written to the tastes of academics like Seymour and old-money sponsors such as Harry Day, William Farnam, and Henry Townshend. He also had a measured sense of the capacities of city government. He doubtless considered a full-scale implementation of the report to be well beyond those capacities. The required coordination between city departments would become a nightmare of bureaucratic politics.

In 1916, Mayor Frank Rice died and Richard C. Lee was born. Elected mayor in 1953, Lee would form a citizen's action commission and would establish a supply line of federal dollars to support its urban renewal program for New Haven. This project, or jumble of projects, would lack the unity of vision Seymour had sought and the balanced sensibility of the Gilbert and Olmsted report. Lee, while motivated by many of the same concerns that fueled the 1910 Plan, such as the chaos and congestion of the old industrial city and the persistent preoccupation with the movement of traffic, would now turn to planning models in the modernist vocabulary of his consultants and advisers, trading, for example, the "emerald necklace" of parks and parkways of the 1910 Plan for limited-access ring roads and connectors to be built with federal highway dollars. We now find ourselves attempting to undo some of the damage wrought by that latest generation of master planning and, as we do so, turning back to the unfinished work of the 1910 Plan.

NOTES

1 George Dudley Seymour, *New Haven* (1942).

2 Clarence H. Ryden, *New Haven of Today* (1892), 42.

3 Federal Energy Regulation Commission data consistently place Greater New Haven in the top one-half percent of electric utility costs.

4 *New Haven Chronicle*, December 31, 2010. Quoted in Douglas W. Rae, *City: Urbanism and Its End* (New Haven: Yale University Press, 2003), 206.

5 Seymour, *New Haven*